PRAISE FOR *ENERGY HEA*

⤳

"This book, by itself, can unleash your natural healing abilities and teach you to become an effective healer—a remarkable achievement."
—LEONARD LASKOW, M.D., author of *Healing With Love: A Breakthrough Mind/Body Medical Program for Healing Yourself and Others*

"*Energy Healing* is a 'must read' for those who practice energy healing and for those wishing to learn about and engage in such practices. It is written from a wise and balanced perspective, and points out both the extreme benefits that can be achieved through energy medicine and healing, and some of the crucial pitfalls that may be encountered. Written in a well-organized, interesting, and clear manner, it sets a tone for personal growth and responsible practice. I highly recommend this book."
—ANN NUNLEY, 1998–99 co-president, International Society for the Study of Subtle Energies & Energy Medicine (ISSSEEM) and author of *Inner Counselor* and *Landscapes of the Heart*

"*Energy Healing* is an excellent, practical sourcebook that brings powerful healing tools down from the mountaintop into our living rooms. I'm particularly impressed with the spiritual foundation work that Gilkeson gives the budding healer. I can't wait to offer this book to the clients and practitioners at my healing center."
—PAUL SIBCY, author of *Healing Your Rift With God: A Guide to Spiritual Renewal and Ultimate Healing* and co-founder of Integrated Healing Arts and Pathways to Self-Healing, holistic clinics in Palo Alto, California

"*Energy Healing* is an exciting, inspiring, and invigorating addition to the field. Written by a gifted teacher and master clinician, Jim offers the reader a combination of substantial investigation, folksy wisdom, and enough provocative experiences for a lifetime, or two."
—RICHARD A. HECKLER, Ph.D., director of the Hakomi Insitute and author of *Crossings: Everyday People, Unexpected Events, and Life-Affirming Change*

"Jim Gilkeson is a true poet in the language of the body. His gentle wisdom challenges our perceptions about the many levels of illness and healing, and opens our eyes and hearts to miraculous possibilities. This book is a healing gift for anyone seeking the secrets of healing energy."
—WAYNE MULLER, author of *How, Then, Shall We Live?:*
Four Simple Questions and *Legacy of the Heart:*
The Spiritual Advantages of a Painful Childhood

"Reading this outstanding book is like taking a comprehensive course in the theory and practice of subtle-energy healing. Jim Gilkeson has created a highly informative and highly practical guide accessible to just about anyone."

—JEFF LEVIN, Ph.D., M.P.H., past president, International Society for the Study of Subtle Energies & Energy Medicine (ISSSEEM)

"*Energy Healing* is a book which will surely become a 'must' for all engaged in selfgrowth and healing. Comprehensive, thorough, and clearly stated, it is a healer's textbook. Yet it is also more than this—it is a shared journey, full of personal experience and completely free from pomposity. The language is clear, creative, and *fun*. It offers an abundance of practical, sound exercises for those developing sensitivity and their ability to heal themselves and others. These exercises are clearly described and the participant feels cared for when undertaking them, because no stages are missed and transitions from subtle experience to the normal world are well handled. I would not hesitate to recommend this book to anyone exploring or training in the world of healing."
—RUTH WHITE, psychotherapist, healer, channel, and author
of *Chakras: A New Approach to Healing Your Life*
and *The River of Life: A Guide to Your Spiritual Journey*

"*Energy Healing* is a workbook that not only provides healing exercises but also personal guidance throughout the process. Drawing upon his own lifelong quest for spiritual, mental, and physical health, Jim Gilkeson shares the wealth of his own experiences with wit and wisdom."

—DENISE LOW, Ph.D., author of *Tulip Elegies:*
An Alchemy of Writing and *Touching the Sky*

ENERGY
HEALING

ENERGY
HEALING

A PATHWAY TO
INNER GROWTH

JIM GILKESON

Foreword by Hal Zina Bennett
Illustrations by Beth Budesheim

MARLOWE & COMPANY
NEW YORK

Published by
Marlowe & Company
841 Broadway, 4th Floor
New York, NY 10003

Permissions appear on page 207 and constitute a continuation of the copyright page.

The practices in this book are not intended to be a substitute for care
by a qualified health professional. If you have questions about how these practices
will affect your physical, emotional or mental condition,
please consult your doctor before doing them.

Library of Congress Cataloging-in-Publication Data
Gilkeson, Jim
Energy healing / by Jim Gilkeson.
p. cm.
Includes bibliographical references.
ISBN 1-56924-655-6
1. Alternative medicine. 2. Therapeutics, Suggestive. 3. Mind and body. I. Title.
R733 .G54 2000
615.8'52—dc21

99-045858

DESIGNED BY PAULINE NEUWIRTH, NEUWIRTH & ASSOCIATES
Manufactured in the United States of America
Distributed by Publishers Group West

10 9 8 7 6 5 4 3

THIS BOOK IS DEDICATED WITH LOVE TO
Ursula Gilkeson,
my wife and partner, and a healer of special gifts,
my first teacher in energywork,

❧

AND TO
Bob Moore,
our teacher of, lo, these many years.
Bob has demonstrated in his unadorned way that,
more than any technique or information, the essence of
healer education is development of the heart and feeling for people.
I come back again and again to his example.

❧

AND IN LOVING MEMORY OF MY PARENTS,
Frances Comstock Hurd Gilkeson and *Hunter Boyd Gilkeson, Jr.*

CONTENTS

❧

OPENING TALK: THE HEALER'S PREDICAMENT   5

This "opening talk" addresses the challenge of discovering and
developing your healing gifts as well as the particular situation
of those who sense that their path as a healer is intertwined
with their spiritual path. Also addressed is the shift in orientation from symptom to transformation of the individual which
energy healing necessitates.

❧

FIRST ETHERIC LABORATORY:

EXPERIENCING THE PRESENCE OF ENERGY   17

This Laboratory presents important first steps in the practice of energy healing, namely, our ability to directly experience the medium we are to work in. This laboratory chapter provides you with personal exercises for becoming familiar with the etheric, the aspect of your energy field which immediately surrounds and penetrates your physical body.

❦

SECOND ETHERIC LABORATORY:
ENERGY-ACTIVE POSITIONS ON THE BODY   53

This Laboratory acquaints you with some of the stable features of the subtle energetic anatomy which come into play in energy healing work; introduces a simple but effective energy healing treatment.

THIRD ETHERIC LABORATORY: THE ENERGY KIVA   73

The subject of this Laboratory is the energetic environment in which you do your healing work, stressing the role of safety, containment and energetic alignment and expansion of consciousness in healing. A useful "first-aid" treatment is introduced.

FOURTH ETHERIC LABORATORY:
HEALING THE ETHERIC   87

This Laboratory acquaints you with the many factors that affect the etheric, giving us clues as to how it can be healed. Personal exercises are introduced for the deep exploration of the etheric and how to heal blockage that impedes its free movement.

FIFTH ETHERIC LABORATORY:

Part I of this Laboratory provides a profile of each chakra, its
functions, polarities and potential problems. Part 2 provides
you with a means of working in a healing way with your individual chakras and Part 3 focuses on the important role of the
lower chakras and provides exercises specially designed for
their healing.

SIXTH ETHERIC LABORATORY:

This Laboratory is about the role of physical and emotional release in healing. Energy exercises with a "release phase" are introduced. A final healing exercise is provided which combines most elements introduced in this book.

CLOSING TALK: PROGRESSIVE HEALING:

This "closing talk" takes up the subject of "progressive healing," that is, healing which brings us forward, into a "new place" in our lives. We will look at the tendency of energy healing to introduce new impulses from higher dimensions of consciousness and produce profound progressive change. Central to this chapter is a new look at the role played by the principle of polarity in healing.

FOREWORD

IN THE 1970s I wrote a book called *The Well Body Book* with Mike Samuels, a doctor friend of mine. For its time, it was revolutionary, if not downright subversive. Besides promoting the idea that each of us should be the final authority about our bodies and our health, it talked about alternative healing modes. Energy healing was one of the subjects we took on.

Though we'd never intended to be controversial I'm afraid we caused quite a stir. When we lectured around the country, physicians often attacked us. "Where medicine is concerned," they argued, "a *little* knowledge can be dangerous." We countered by saying, "But *no knowledge can be disastrous!*"

We were taken to task for promoting meditation, visualization, yoga, physical exercise, acupuncture, nutrition, as well as personal and spiritual development, as health-enhancing tools. None of these, the experts told us, had been proven to have any impact whatsoever on health. Today we would find such statements laughable but at the time we had only our own intuition and collection of anecdotal "proofs" to argue our case. So, we mostly didn't argue.

The attacks were not always comfortable, particularly for my co-author whose profession was at stake. Nevertheless, we stood our ground. At times we grew pessimistic and even questioned if perhaps we really were the "flakes" we were being accused of being. Then the tides turned. Five years after *The Well Body Book* came out, we began hearing from doctors who were buying copies of our books for their patients, or otherwise making them available to the public. They were showing up in bookstores at medical schools, and even being adopted for nursing courses. Mike, with his M.D., found himself in demand, speaking at medical conventions around the country.

Medicine and the public's awareness of health was radically changing. More and more people were seeking out health-enhancing tools
ranging from massage to psychic healing. The total faith that we had
once placed in science to cure all our ills was shifting. We were seeing
the limits of modern medicine and were turning back to take another look at healing practices that were, in some cases, tens of thousands
of years old.

Even as huge, profit-oriented corporations take over health care in
America—or maybe because of it—interest in healing continues to
grow. Health clinics and hospitals connected to some of the greatest
medical schools are including "complementary and alternative medicine" in their lists of services.

How seriously are these alternative and complementary modes
being taken? In 1992, the Office of Alternative Medicine (OAM) was
established by a Congressional mandate and soon afterwards became
part of the National Institutes of Health. Then, in 1998, again by
Congressional mandate, the National Center for Complementary &
Alternative Medicine came into being. Their purpose was to research
and facilitate alternative medical treatments and provide the public
with information about them. Today, they also serve as a referral
agency for alternative treatments and practitioners. (Check it out on
the web: http://nccam.nih.gov.) Their annual budget has swelled from
$2 million in 1993 to $50 million for 1999!

I'd say that we've come a long way since *The Well Body Book* days!

So what does all this have to do with Jim Gilkeson and this wonderful book, *Energy Healing,* which you hold in your hands? A lot, I
think. Jim is one of a growing number of health practitioners in this
country whose lives were changed by energy healing. While it is true
that he is in the *avant garde* of alternative medicine, his experience, his
dedication and his expertise have already made their mark. He knows
of what he speaks not just because he has studied energy healing but
because he has experienced it firsthand, as a healer, as a patient, and
as a gifted teacher showing others how to integrate these techniques
in their own lives.

While there are dozens of books which talk about energywork, in
all its various forms, from acupuncture to Zero Balancing, most have
done so in a theoretical way. Being a bodyworker and energyworker,
Jim realized that there was a certain irony about trying to teach peo-

ple about this work by words alone. And so he took a quantum leap beyond what most others were doing. He incorporated into his writing instructions for experiential exercises that would allow readers not just to read about energy but feel first hand how it manifests and moves through their bodies.

By daring what he has dared in this book, Jim takes those who sincerely want to know about energy healing beyond the comfort zones of their own lives. If you are one of those who is willing to do that, to take the time and effort it will require, you will be rewarded a thousand-fold.

I can think of very few journeys more rewarding, for in the process a whole world opens up. Some of the mysteries of the life force itself come to light, not reducing them to principles but taking you right inside them until you swell with awe. It's a journey that takes you into the unknown, presenting new potentials that are virtually guaranteed to change the way you experience your life.

Like so many people who are committing their lives to healing, Jim is a humble person, not one to beat his own drum. However, I'd like to say that what he has assembled here is an extraordinary accomplishment. He has distilled into these pages not a patented system of healing that puts him on a pedestal but something much more valuable. He offers tools that put the wisdom and power of this information directly into the reader's consciousness. I believe there is no more generous or important teaching than that.

Whether you are a health practitioner looking to broaden your horizons or a person seeking healing, you will find miracles enough in these pages. One book, no matter how comprehensive, will never be enough, of course. But as Lao-tzu once advised, "A journey of a thousand miles must begin with a single step."

What better first step than this?

—*Hal Zinna Bennett, M.S., Ph.D.*

HAL ZINA BENNETT, M.S., PH.D. is the author of 28 books, including the ground-breaking *Well Body Book,* which sadly is no longer in print. His most recent work is *Spirit Circle,* a fictional work that explores yet another form of ancient healing: shamanism.

A Note to the Reader

MUCH EFFORT HAS gone into making *Energy Healing: A Pathway to Inner Growth* as readable as possible, hopefully creating a down-to-earth book about a not so down-to-earth topic. Here are some tips on getting the most out of this book.

Of course this book can be read from beginning to end, but each section can also be read as a separate unit, so please feel free to roam about and find what is useful to you. The Table of Contents includes a short description of what you can expect to find in each chapter. It was my hope to provide you in this way with a small "map" of the book.

Each of the "Etheric Laboratories" that make up the middle of the book starts with a discussion of an important topic in energy healing, followed by one or more experiential practices which illustrate energy principles. In most cases, these are energy exercises for self-healing which you can do by yourself. The second and third Etheric Laboratories feature energy healing practices which you do with a partner.

The exercises you will find in the Etheric Laboratories are the meat of the book. They will carry you over the line that divides the actual *practice* of energywork from merely reading about it. Before undertaking any of the exercises, I encourage you to carefully read the section entitled Structure and Discipline of Experiential Exercises, which will help you to get the most out of these practices and do them safely.

I have named the six experiential sections "Etheric Laboratories" for a couple of reasons. A "laboratory" suggests a clean, well-lighted place where we carry out our experiments, find out for ourselves what works, and what doesn't. The "etheric," in this case, refers to the particular aspect of our energy field that we will be working with in most of the exercises presented in this book. It immediately surrounds our physical bodies and plays a vital role in energy healing. Luckily, it is relatively easy to learn to feel this part of our energy field. The instruction in this book is aimed at becoming familiar with the etheric and mobilizing its potentials for our health and inner growth.

The writing of this book has been a joyful adventure for me. The practices I describe have been useful to me and others, and I hope they will be for you, too. I wish you all the best in your healing journey.

—J.G.

ACKNOWLEDGMENTS

As Hillary Clinton said, "it takes a village. . . ." This book does not exist in a vacuum. I would never have come to the point of writing if not for the community of people that populate this writing. I owe a tremendous debt of gratitude to a number of people:

Bob Moore and my wife, Ursula Gilkeson, for being my main teachers in energy healing—without them, I would not have had anything to write;

Antje Martin, Denise Low and Sue Gilkeson for their repeated encouragement to write this book;

Sonja Becker-Hiemer for an indelible image;

Brent Flanders for his generous expert help in times of computer crisis;

Anita Birnberger for her verses and open ear;

Diane Tegtmeier, Denise Low, Mary Howe, Jim Roberts, Ken Lassman, Jennifer Sullivan, Sharon Conden and Barbara Salvini for critiquing the first draft of this manuscript;

Beth Budesheim, who illustrated these pages, for the talent, creativity and perseverance she brought to this project; Beth and I would both like to extend our heartfelt thanks to all our models: Lloyd duPont, Cathy King, Caroline King, Korey Ireland, Rachel Creager, Alison Smith and Annie Magill;

My colleagues at the Southwind Health Collective for their continued support;

My clients and all the people who have participated in our workshops over the years for their trust and their interest.

My sincere thanks goes to Matthew Lore, Senior Editor at Marlowe & Company, for his enthusiastic support and belief in this project. It was a dream come true the October evening in 1998 when he called and picked my brain about my book proposal.

And I want to express my deepest gratitude to Hal Zina Bennett, who together with his wife Susan Sparrow mentored me through the intense months of revising this manuscript. Their editorial skill and wisdom is in every page of this book. When Hal told me that they were actually trying to *do* the treatments and exercises in order to figure out what in the world I was talking about, I knew I was in good hands.

I am also grateful to Joseph Campbell, Thomas Merton and Samuel Lewis, who, though I never had the privilege of meeting them in person, have affected my life in strange and wonderful ways.

ILLUSTRATIONS LIST

Put coarse-chunked salt in a skillet,
turn up the heat and watch it
sweat and spit.
A droplet of water is hiding
in every molecule of salt.
When crusty foursquare molecules melt,
salt weeps for newfound freedom.
Where does that water want to go?

The Little Mermaid traded her tongue for legs
to walk on land
and be with her sailor. Now she's
stuck in Copenhagen
without a ticket home, frozen
in bronze, staring out to sea. Shall we
break open that statue
and let her out?

Bittersweet longing of a drop of water
for the ocean.

ENERGY
HEALING

INTRODUCTION

IN MY WORK as a healthcare practitioner I am always finding people who are curious about the human energy field and its role in healing, personal growth and spiritual development. Sometimes I have the time to sit down with them and share or demonstrate some of its potentials. Often, however, I feel frustrated because we don't have time to explore this fascinating subject together. So, in an effort to answer the questions of friends, clients, other health practitioners, and students who have attended my seminars, I offer the information and exercises in the following pages.

At first I was not so convinced that a book was the ideal way to share this information, since I believe that we need to personally experience how energy works, not just read about it. But I have since come to believe that by providing exercises that readers could do on their own, they would be able to do just that: experience it for themselves. I think you'll find that you can read about and experience the energywork exercises contained in this book at whatever pace is comfortable for you.

In writing these pages I have, of course, made certain assumptions about you, the reader. Perhaps you are a massage therapist, a body-worker, a healthcare practitioner, a nurse or a physician, and you have become interested in touch therapies. You might even be one of that rare breed of surgeons who are getting interested in the role of subtle energy in healing.

Maybe you are a spiritual seeker who is attracted to energy-influencing disciplines, such as meditation and chakra work, because you see them as ways to deepen your appreciation of life, expand your consciousness, and cultivate your spiritual gifts.

Wherever you stand in the broad spectrum of practitioners, healers and others who are exploring the role of energy in healing, I think you will find this book helpful. Energywork can be approached from many directions. It would be naïve of me to assume that everyone begins such a journey from the same perspective.

Maybe you are a person who is facing physical, emotional or spiritual challenges of your own, or you have a loved one who is facing such challenges, and you are looking for solutions that conventional medicine, psychotherapy or even religion seem unable to provide.

If you are a bodyworker, you might have spent years nailing down solid fundamentals and techniques in an established healing discipline, and now you are adding energy-oriented techniques that are compatible with your work.

If you operate on a more intuitive basis, having perhaps become aware of psychic gifts—an ability to lay your hands on another person in a healing way, for example, or an ability to sense the energy field—you might find in this book a way to gain a grounded understanding of what is taking place.

What you'll be exploring here is healing in general, and energywork in particular. This means you will be focusing on the knowledgeable use of the energy field that surrounds and penetrates the human body, and what it has to do with healing and personal growth. Look over the Table of Contents and you'll get a pretty good idea of the broad range of material you'll be covering here—from basic information about subtle energy to meditative personal self-healing practices and healing treatments that can be practiced with a partner. In order to give readers as comprehensive a look as possible at energywork, I've included discussions and exercises about everything from the ancient study of the chakras and other energy-active positions on the body to the subtle influences of color, sound, imagery and geometric form.

You may find that what you read in these pages will challenge what you presently believe about physical reality and our power to effect change. Because of this, the experiential exercises offered here are particularly important. Remember, you are going to be working with a non-physical reality that does not easily translate into words or broad generalizations. Most of us cannot see energy with the naked eye, nor can we weigh it or put it in our pocket. However, we can certainly tell when it is present and when it isn't. A friend offered this explanation—that the presence of energy is what allows us to distinguish between a live chicken and a dead one. The bottom line is that your firsthand experience of energywork will reveal truths that your intellect may very well have to grapple with.

I would like to think that this book will help readers establish a foundation for thinking about and starting to work with energy for healing and personal growth. This is not a "patented method" or dogma of healing; rather, it brings together a rich collection of the more teachable aspects of healing and energywork. Once that foundation is established you will discover on your own that you might be inspired to go further. That might include seeking out teachers with specific systems that you can either adopt or adapt for your own use.

Over the past twenty years, we have seen an explosion in the therapeutic use of practices that have been integral to spiritual and esoteric disciplines for thousands of years. Meditation, yoga practice, acupuncture, acupressure, and bio-energetic exercises are now commonplace in holistic practices and clinics everywhere. It sometimes seems that no issue of the leading women's magazines and new age magazines is without health articles signaling yet another re-emergence of "ancient wisdom" which can be employed as health and beauty aids.

Current interest in energywork has fortunately, or unfortunately, been centered around its therapeutic aspects. Subtle energy practices (which are essentially spiritual practices) definitely can be used in this way, for example, in physical therapy or stress reduction. There is nothing wrong with using them for such purposes, but we should never overlook the fact that energywork comes from spiritual tradition. To view them exclusively as a way to control symptoms is tantamount to asking a famous neurosurgeon to perform a pedicure or having access to the world's greatest library and then limiting yourself to a single book from all of its rich selections. The point is that energywork, by its nature, brings us face to face with the spiritual, and by limiting its use to therapy we overlook the vast wisdom that it offers.

The blending of psychology and spirituality has gained increasing recognition over the past thirty years—known in many circles as "transpersonal psychology." By bringing these two ways of working together, we raise the possibility of addressing a greater totality of our lives as well as acknowledging spiritual development as a critical part of human development. This trend tells us that there is broadening validation for this area of study, even in the relatively conservative field of mainstream psychology.

As you go along, you will no doubt discover my own excitement about energywork, as well as my convictions about its power for inner growth and spiritual development. Whatever it is that has piqued your interest in energy healing, if it is accompanied by your desire to learn about yourself and a feeling for helping other people, I am sure that you will find this book helpful.

The intention behind this book is to help you to organize a practical means of working with the energy field in self-healing and in your personal development. My fondest wish is that these pages might expand the horizons of your awareness, provide you with a foundation for your personal development, and point to ways that you might bring the fruits of that development to others.

OPENING TALK
THE HEALER'S PREDICAMENT

THE DISCOVERY THAT you have healing gifts, along with the discovery that you suffer if you don't find a way to express them, can be a rather lonely discovery. It can be hard to talk about, even to yourself. Of course, many people with healing gifts find their way into established healing professions as doctors, nurses, therapists and counselors, and these jobs seem to be a good match. Others travel a long way in this life with the abiding sense that though they might even find themselves in a "healing profession," their true vocation in healing is "none of the above."

The path of the healer is not necessarily satisfied by any of the conventional roles mainstream society offers. This is particularly confusing if you sense that your healing gifts cannot be separated from your own inner growth or your spiritual path. By this I do not mean to suggest a romanticized Hollywood image of the spiritual healer walking through hospital wards in a nimbus of light, laying hands on the sick and dying, who then jump up and shout "Hallelujah!"

The popular image of the healer can be so inflated or so bizarre that we can hardly imagine being one ourselves. When I was ten years old I used to listen to the evangelist healers on a late-night radio station blasting up from just across the Mexican border. Late at night, with my tiny transistor radio pressed tightly to my ear, a pillow wrapped around my head and the radio to muffle the sounds, I would hear Brother Al or some other radio preacher ask if you had "the miseries in your back, or kidney problems in your stomach" or if you needed money. He then invited listeners to "place one hand on the radio, and one hand on the afflicted place, and pray with me the prayer of faith!" After which he spoke in tongues—on a school night!—for fifteen minutes. While this radio healer may have fascinated me, it clearly was not an image I could identify with as a healer.

Who's a healer? The popular image of the "healer" is so inflated that it can sound unbearably immodest to claim to be one. When we use the word "healer" it seems to imply that some of us are healers, while the rest of us aren't. But healing potential exists in each of us. It would be fair to say that this particular quality in a healer is not only a potential but is consciously developed, active and strong. First and foremost, it is important to recognize that it is not so much that the "healer" heals another person, but rather that he triggers the other person's own self-healing potential.

Some people who understand that they have genuine healing qualities can get so puffed up in their image of themselves as healers that they need to undergo some kind of ego bypass operation before they are able to do anybody any good. Or they might go in the opposite direction and get caught up in false modesty, saying to themselves, "who am I to presume to be a healer?" When that happens, they end up neglecting gifts that they actually have. There is, therefore, a need to back off from the inflated, heroic images of the healer, while still *doing* something to help these qualities—it is not inappropriate to call them spiritual gifts—to express.

Healer Education

While some people glide serenely into the active expression of their gifts, others may find them an unwelcome burden in an already complicated life and view them as anything but a welcome gift. Those who are seriously drawn to spiritual development and healing are often sensitive people who have their hands full trying to marshal dimensions of life that most folks are not even aware of. They might find that, while everybody else seems to be doing just fine, they themselves have to deal with a highly sensitive body, mood swings that go off the scale, intuitions that fly in the face of good old logic, perhaps an ability to pick up on other people's thoughts and emotions (whether they want to pick up on them or not), assorted impressions coming to them from who knows where. They might discover that they are highly intuitive, anticipating events, phone calls, encounters and the like. Some have unwanted "power surges" which they struggle to bring under control. They might go through periods of being energetic "loose cannons," leaving a trail of stopped wrist watches, broken china, and broken hearts in their wake. They can go through phases of being strident, overly intense, and unpleasant to be around until compassion enters their hearts and they soften and open up.

When groups of people with the gift of healing get together, anything can happen, some of it quite disruptive. Such experiences offer evidence for their capacity to affect the etheric dimensions but more than anything else it demonstrates the need to school these abilities and develop positive disciplines for their application in healing. Anyone who has ever been involved with an esoteric school can attest to this. On certain days, fuses blow, literally and figuratively, with the scattered vectors of undisciplined energy. Meanwhile, the most effective healers and spiritual adepts are those who have learned to manage themselves, sort out their spiritual gifts and dedicate themselves to service.

My own early lessons in this came to a head on a New Year's Eve in Rome. In earlier times, it was the New Year's custom in Italy to throw all the crockery in the house out the window at the stroke of midnight—out with the old and in with the new—but that all ended soon after the invention of automobiles and pneumatic tires. Our zany New Year's celebration was in the home of Signora Alda DeLucia, a poet and mystic and mother of a colleague of mine from a spiritual order we both belonged to. Twenty of us ate, drank, sang, and danced in long, snaking lines through the rooms of the apartment. After midnight, we calmed down somewhat. I helped to wash the dishes and when I very gently picked up a crystal fruit bowl to dry it—gently because I knew it was an old piece—it shattered with a startling crack! in my hands.

I felt terrible about this, but Alda, being a Roman Lady, took it in stride. Some weeks later, I received a poem from her in the mail which shook me up. The poem was an ode to that crystal bowl, a family heirloom, generations old, and ended with words to this effect: ". . . and hands, which should be busy healing, broke it." It marked the beginning of of a slow turning in me toward a realization that although I may have latent gifts, they had to be developed in order to be used safely and responsibly. That experience grew into a desire to learn the ropes.

Learning to Manage the Tools of Your Trade

This brings us to the notion of using tools and practices to cultivate our healer qualities. Though the potential for healing may be present in all of us, its positive expression requires a parallel spiritual development. Without a deep respect for the spiritual links between ourselves and the infinite dimensions of life, what can and should be a comfort in our lives can be quite the opposite; our gift can turn on us and cause harm. For most healers, there comes a point in their lives when their growth stops being exclusively personal and they begin seeking ways to use their deeper qualities to benefit others.

For many years, I have been intensely interested in the education of healers. Many people with the gift of healing find themselves resisting this idea. I have heard healers say, "I'm afraid that if I get too structured, it will clog up my intuition" or "I'm afraid I'll get too left-brained." But healing requires both intuition *and* rational knowledge. Flying by the seat of your intuitive pants into someone's energy system, though it can bring about fascinating results, often leaves both you and your treatment partners without any insight and without any long-term benefits. On the contrary, there is potential for long-term damage! There is something to be said for knowing something. Education allows intuition, understanding, and respect for the powers of healing and its deeper dimensions to blend.

I went back to college some years ago. To finish off my requirements for my degree, I had to take a course in logic. After all the time I had spent trying to cultivate my intuition, I prepared myself for a "learning experience" (the all-American euphemism for something I knew I was going to hate). The logic course involved the process of straight-line, leave-no-step-out sequential thinking in the form of the Nineteen Inference Rules of Logic. With all these calisthenics for the left hemisphere of the brain, I figured that my intuition would more or less atrophy. But I found instead that, like any good partnership, the marriage of intuition and the capacity for analysis makes both parties stronger and more useful. Far from losing my intuitive antennae, I found that my attunement and creativity *increased* in that time. The experience suggested that the supposedly separate functions of analysis and intuition are unified functions of the same mind.

Structured learning and spontaneous intuition are not really at war with one another. Indeed, *factual understanding creates a pole toward which intuition can move.* The more truly differentiated our knowledge base and the more tools it has at its disposal, the greater the variety of our intuitive repertoire. The healer-in-training learns the names of things, develops skills, sensitivity, and a broad acquaintance with a number of fields of knowledge, from science to religion and art, from psychology to anatomy and physiology.

The education of a healer consists of input from many different sources, traditional and non-traditional. Traditional learning comes from all that has been handed down from past generations, and from the particular habits, lore, and wisdom of our culture. Non-traditional learning comes from our own direct "fall down and go BOOM!" experience, as well as ecstatic states in which we transcend experience. One thing has become abundantly clear to me, however: healer education needs to provide, alongside factual knowledge, opportunities to gain direct, first-hand experience. Since we are so often working outside consensus reality we need to be able to draw from resources that we ourselves hold within us, and learn how to trust them.

The Dilemma of the Modern Spiritual Initiate

For centuries the subtle energy practices of the healer have been harbored within a carefully guarded esoteric tradition. They were formerly available only to those who were schooled in the spiritual. This meant that healer education was the domain of people who were methodically educated in the classic disciplines of the inner life: meditation, contemplation and prayer. And for good reason! The fact is that there is nothing subtle about "subtle" energy. The stable features of the energy system, such as chakras and energy points, are intrapsychic portals, gateways to dimensions of great power. When activated, they can have tremendous impact on the human psyche and, through the psyche, can have a dramatic effect on the physical body. For that reason, if no other, we need to think of energywork as essentially a spiritual practice, whether we call it that or not.

By placing our intentions and attention on these energetic realms of consciousness, we are invoking the powers of Heaven and the changes which that brings. When we do that, a wealth of unconscious material that we may not have known existed can bubble to the surface of our psyches, while at the same time we open ourselves to receive energy and information from higher dimensions.

Are all of these changes and openings that can take place in energy healing good? Are they truly beneficial in terms of healing? Persons schooled and knowledgeable in these dimensions recognize that though these events are challenging, they are hallmarks of deep inner transformation, and so they welcome the times when they occur. Still, when we are in the thick of such processes, we might awaken in the wee hours of the night to find our angels and our demons mud-wrestling in our living rooms. If we're to successfully negotiate this process, we need to prepare ourselves physically, emotionally and conceptually. We become increasingly aware of why the healing arts were once fiercely guarded within a spiritual tradition where each healer learned to negotiate the etheric dimensions.

We live in a profoundly secular society, separated from those religions and spiritual traditions that once schooled healers in the wisdom of the ages. Yet people are undergoing initiation of a spiritual nature in the inner chambers of their own lives. Nowadays, in many people, spiritual initiation is a spontaneous, organic process; their life experiences create a kind of intrapsychic "critical mass" that opens them to spiritual realms. Without our asking, our stars line up, so to speak, and we pass over a threshold of change. No elder or ritual master has "removed the scales from our eyes," as the Bible says, yet we may pass through authentic changes at a very deep spiritual level.

The problem is that the modern initiate is often left to his own devices, unaware that there are known patterns to these experiences. In our role as healers it is important to realize that we, as well as those we treat, may be going through initiation processes that are powerful and profound. For that reason, it is critical that we appreciate this transformative process, beginning with how we ourselves are affected by it.

We don't have an everyday language about spiritual initiation. Still, that process is much more universal and diversified than most people believe. Initiation in the spiritual sense can loosely be defined as any experience which would make a person change their ways and live according to a higher order. For example, at midlife, a woman with a highly successful legal career witnesses a bad car accident on her way home from the office. That night she awakens from a dream, suddenly aware of how fragile and vulnerable each human life truly is. She reflects on her own life, and though she is wildly successful by society's measures, she feels profoundly dissatisfied. Two weeks later she sells her practice, not knowing her next move but aware of spiritual truths that she feels she must pursue.

Spontaneous initiation processes in this sense typically involve learning life's lessons, such as the limits of our mortality, or how the intentions we hold in our minds can affect the world around us. No doubt we are provided with plenty of opportunities to face and overcome our fears, mobilize our latent strengths and move beyond what we have known. In its most basic form, spontaneous initiatory openings to the etheric and spiritual realms involve a passage into a new state of being, giving rise to very different ways of viewing our lives and the world around us.

What I observe in my own life, and especially in my healing practice, is that our development often follows the classic threefold spiritual path: leaving the world; going into a sacred space; then returning to the world in a changed state with something to offer the world. This pattern is repeated in every meditation, treatment and retreat. We see it in the background of every instance of authentic personal change. It is the process which moves us forward in our own evolution.

A Shift in Goal-Setting

There is a growing awareness in this country that subtle energy practices can shorten healing time for damaged tissue, shorten recovery time after operations, reduce side-effects of radiation and chemotherapy, and help to manage pain. They definitely should be used in these situations, for they can bring great comfort to millions of people. Yet it is important, particularly for people just entering the field of energy healing, to grapple with certain issues that arise in the process.

Understand that if we narrow our use of energy healing practices to the physiological level, we may be ignoring the fact that these are primarily consciousness-shifting practices. While they may be effective for what some perceive as a purely physical matter, such as reducing convalescent time and managing pain, we should not overlook the fact that we may also be affecting those whom we treat in other ways. In fact, even the most superficial applications of energy healing can't help but affect the person on an energetic level, even if the only reason they chose the healing was to manage a physical symptom.

> *The purpose of learning to work with the unconscious is not just to resolve our conflicts or deal with our neuroses. We find there a deep source of renewal, growth, strength, and wisdom. We connect with the source of our evolving character; we cooperate with the process whereby we bring the total self together; we learn to tap that rich lode of energy and intelligence that waits within.*
>
> ROBERT A. JOHNSON

Subtle energy practices are not really in their own element when employed strictly for fixing problems. If we use these practices in that manner, we might get more than we asked for. Old issues and emotional wounds may bubble forth in your treatment partner, demanding attention. She may have questions about relationships with loved ones that she had never paid much attention to before. Inner conflicts or great clearings of old discord may be experienced. All these may appear random or serendipitous to the person to whom they are happening, but they are anything but that. They only appear that way because the energy healing technique was only employed for the single goal of bringing comfort or speeding a healing process.

Conversely, when energy healing is employed with multi-dimensional goals it is really in its own element. Such goals might range from self-exploration and a search for understanding of what might be behind our illness, to a quest for insight, growth, and wisdom about the totality of our lives. Likewise, energy healing can set in motion a change of consciousness that can transport us from a strictly self-centered, personal focus to a perspective of compassion and a felt sense of interconnection with all of humanity, the natural world, and the cosmos.

The sacred healing arts and sciences have always dealt with what links the body with the soul, and the soul with God. If we insist on calling the use of spiritual practices "therapeutic," then we are talking about a higher octave of therapy, in which the "goal-setting" is different. Spiritually active therapy might not achieve some of the things that we set out to accomplish—for example, it could fail to relieve all physical pain—but might unlock a personal breakthrough from a psychological or spiritual point of view. Spiritually active therapies can help us to enter what might simply be called the "meaningful dimension of life," opening the possibility of going into something completely unknown, completely new, where we do not know what is going to happen. It might be very unsettling.

From Problems, to Exploration, to Transpersonal Experience

None of this is meant to imply that unless a spiritual agenda is announced and carried out, we are missing the boat. It is not my intention to devalue anyone's motives for going to a healer for help. There are no "wrong reasons" for going, though I can think of examples of persons who have had expectations of healers that could not be fulfilled. In my practice, I work daily with people who come predominately with physical problems, and I work to provide, as best I can, some physical relief.

I believe it is, however, important for all of us who are doing this work, or who are seeking the help of energyworkers, to be aware of the wide range of human experiences that energywork encompasses. The energy healer participates in a healing continuum that runs from the direst and most acute problems, such as pain, or providing complementary backup for a person recovering from surgery, all the way to being a "spiritual midwife" in a person's process of enlightenment.

Like anybody else, I will seek relief from any acute problem I might be suffering, and the quicker I can get help the better. And along the way I don't want any nonsense about how pain relief is somehow less worthy because it is supposedly not spiritual. If the problem becomes chronic and comes repeatedly, I also want relief, but at this point I will likely begin to wonder why the problem keeps coming back. I might look for steps which not only relieve the pain but also give me clues that might help me discover the source of my pain or illness. Is there something I need to understand, a more skillful or more harmonious way of living which I need to learn? At this point, we have shifted our priorities from purely physical relief to looking for primary causes, that is, from the use of energywork for "fixing" to embracing its wider psychological and spiritual range.

Once I become oriented to looking within for insights about the problem I am facing—let's say it's chronic back pain—I might find that there are tools and practices which help me to do this. Subtle energy practice is one of these tools, as it provides a means of shifting my awareness along an entire continuum, from the physical dimension of my life to the spiritual. I might find that besides being confronted with my pain and lack of understanding, there are many other discoveries to be made as well, many new insights into the workings of life—issues I might never have encountered if I had not sought relief and found a broader way of healing my total life, and not just my symptoms.

Therapies that do more than manage symptoms and modify behavior usually try to unveil how we are put together. We get busy, making conscious the forces that shape our experience; we mine the motherlodes of experience and beliefs which shape our life experience. Of course there are some nice by-products of shifting from a strictly problem-solving orientation to a therapy of exploration and discovery, which can include: insights, physical and emotional release, and unburdening, comfort, and nurture, as well as a new confidence. All this is therapeutic in the broadest meaning of that word, and obviously of great value. We might even experience ecstatic moments that go beyond our expectations altogether, expanding our beliefs about what is possible.

None of this supposes that spiritual experience is superior to, or even separate from, say, a migraine headache. Nor are energetic or spiritual orientations better than other orientations. They are, however, *larger,* more all-inclusive categories which operate on a holistic level, embracing body, mind and spirit. That means they include smaller, less-inclusive categories such as the physical body and the emotions. Healers would do well to keep the broadest perspective about what they have to offer every person who seeks their help. Discernment is required; there is a time to work with the small picture and a time to work with the big picture. By its nature, energy healing is a tool for working with the bigger picture.

Verbal communication can be an important aspect of healing work, yet as healers we also need to be aware of its limitations. Ron Kurtz, who developed Hakomi body-centered psychotherapy, points out that our normal style of conversation is geared toward helping along the movement of information *between* people, but not

> *"When I had no wings to fly, you flew to me."*
>
> —ROBERT HUNTER

within a person. Talk therapy can help sort out conscious and near-conscious experience, but as healers we are often working with information that is not conscious at all.

Each person's life is organized on many levels, not all of which are verbal in nature or can be accessed by talking about what we know. Most of us are acquainted with people who can recite a litany of information about themselves. They know their own stories backwards and forwards—or seem to. In our culture, for example, we have developed a rich vocabulary for discussing childhood trauma and sexual injury. In fact, part of the problem with the popularization of these issues has been that millions of people now identify with their wounds so strongly that they will even introduce themselves as a "recovering alcoholic," or an "adult wounded child," or a "recovering sex addict," or whatever the current "new" therapeutic category happens to be. This can make it all too easy to fabricate an identity just as temporary and as far from their core self as what they had when they started their therapy. Trouble is that while this new language is a necessary tool for bringing our inner selves out into the open, it can ultimately create a greater chasm between ourselves and the truth about our lives. After all, we are much more than our childhood wounds. To identify primarily with our wounds is to turn our back on our greatest personal riches.

Spiritual disciplines and subtle energy practices do not exist in order to make the institutions of our lives and cultures more valid,

but rather they serve *in the renewal of an age-old experience*: the opening
of our consciousness to what is often an *incommunicable* dimension of
experience. At least not communicable in terms of doctrine or philosophy, or even words. They are about getting better acquainted with
eternal and universal truths that transcend the realities that we
humans have created. This is something which we can only open to at
the deepest possible level of our being. But to create a pathway into
the deeper, core material that our personalities wrap themselves
around—and then move beyond that personal core—we will have to
do something more than talk about it! We need spiritually active
forms of therapy that can prepare for the shift from problems to a
therapy of exploration to transpersonal experience. Here is where subtle energy practices truly come into their own. They involve discipline; they require practice and perseverance. They reward you, however, by drawing you into experiences of the numinous, mysterious
background of life itself.

At this point in the evolution of a healer, personal growth is no
longer simply personal. What you realize on your own pathway of
inner growth, and the growth of those whose lives you touch as a healer, is ultimately fed back into the consciousness of humanity, to serve
its evolution toward a higher order.

FIRST ETHERIC LABORATORY
EXPERIENCING THE PRESENCE OF ENERGY

FOR THOUSANDS OF years healers and mystics have known that we are surrounded and penetrated by intense subtle activity, dotted with points of pulsating energy and sketched with radiant pathways of energy movement. What is more, they have understood the importance of attending to this energy and tracking its movement throughout the body, along what classic Chinese medicine calls energy meridians. By following these *songlines* of the body, we can be drawn into a seaward voyage toward the hidden but accessible wholeness that makes up each of us.

We can go for the longest time, even meditating regularly and engaging in all kinds of spiritual activities, and never even suspect it is there, this energetic sheath that envelops us. Then one day we "bump into it." Or it is touched just right, activated somehow, and we awaken to something about ourselves which is *not solid.* And yet it is there. Not only is it there, it is *alive.* There is movement in there. It is a place of memory, although it doesn't seem to follow our normal sense of time. It sounds fancy to say that time doesn't exist, but in this energy field around our bodies, our whole personal history is stored; the past is present. Like the annual growth rings inside a tree, each period and phase of life is present just a few layers in.

If you have picked up this book, it is probably fair to make the assumption that you have already recognized the enormous potential of the energetic dimension of life, not only in therapeutic terms, but also in terms of inner growth and spiritual development. Chances are, you have had experiences that brought home to you that the energetic dimension exists, and that it is important. Those experiences aren't as uncommon as one might think. Even if they are only quiet inklings, they mount up until they slip over the line and become a flash of insight, like the magic moment when cold water crystallizes and becomes ice.

You might even remember the first time you had such a moment of insight. For me, it was in 1975. I was driving in the car one evening with a friend named Luke who was describing for me a "psychic surgery" he had witnessed, performed by a Philippine healer. The healer he had watched at quite close range appeared to reach into the body of the person on the table and extract diseased tissue. Even back then, I knew that there was a lot of debate about whether or not such a thing really happens, or whether the healer is merely creating an effective illusion. As Luke continued his description, however, I had to pull the car over to the side of the street as a quick, quiet, but shattering insight broke in on me. I understood, totally independent of Philippine healers or any debates about what they do, that the level that healing happened on was *primarily energetic*. One might say that I experienced in a flash the reality that St. Paul was referring to when he said, "There are also celestial bodies, and bodies terrestrial . . . ." (I Corinthians, 15:40) What Paul didn't mention was that our most immediate contact with our celestial, spiritual body is present through the energy body, which enlivens and informs the physical. What came across to me in Luke's story was that what Paul called the celestial might just be right under our noses, so to speak, through this energetic dimension. At that time, I considered myself to be a spiritually awakened person. I meditated and did daily spiritual practices and had even been initiated into a mystic order. But until that moment, something still had not clicked in me. The celestial and spiritual were still distant, separate from my immediate reality. Samuel Lewis said it's not a matter of when you reach the Kingdom of Heaven, but rather when the Kingdom of Heaven reaches *you*, and something like that happened to me in the car that evening. It changed everything for me.

That moment of realization carried me into a quest for a deeper understanding of energy—how it is expressed in our bodies and how we can perhaps work with it to effect change, personal and spiritual growth, as well as healing. That said, I want to share with you some of the premises that have grown out of this quest for me, premises that have guided the writing of this book, and which continue to evolve and develop:

- *A living energy field surrounds and penetrates our physical bodies.* I assume that most people who are likely to read this book know, at least theoretically, that all life forms have an energy field. There will be no attempt in this book to prove the existence of energy fields. Readers interested in the research on the nature of the human energy field should look into the work of organizations like the International Society for the Study of Subtle Energy and Energy Medicine (ISSSEEM), which host conferences and publish scientific research on all kinds of clinical applications of subtle energy. Dr. Richard Gerber, in his book *Vibrational Medicine: New Choices for Healing Ourselves,* Bear & Company, Santa Fe, 1988, presents the physics of a host of subtle energy techniques, from acupuncture and homeopathy to color therapy and the laying on of hands.
- *The energy field can be experienced.* The same sensory system that we use to be aware of our bodies and our environment can be schooled to sense the human energy field—our own and that of others—and its qualities and movement. Some individuals have an extraordinary capacity for such extended sensory perception.
- Though science has developed instruments with which some aspects of the energy field can be detected and measured, *the deeper study and appreciation of it comes through our own direct experience.*
- *Changes in the energy field precipitate changes in mind, body, emotions, and spirituality, and vice versa.*
- *We can consciously influence the energy field with our attention, thoughts, feelings, and actions.*
- *I assume the essential unity of body, mind, feeling, spirit, and energy field.*
- *We each have qualities, or spiritual gifts, which can be developed.*
- *Healing is an ongoing process,* as opposed to only an end result.
- *Everyone has innate healing potential.* Though the forces of healing may operate unconsciously in most persons, some individuals

develop this potential in ways that apply to healing work with other people.

- *Everybody, whether consciously or unconsciously, has a spirituality which is their relation with the unseen world.* This may or may not find expression in religious forms.
- *The most essential core of our being is a mystery.* The point of our endeavor with energywork is not to demystify, but rather to enter into and embody that mystery.
- *Therapy is enhanced by involvement of the whole person.*
- *Caring makes all the difference.*

To fully grasp the role of energy in our lives, be it in personal development or healing, we need to be able to experience it, rather than just grasp it intellectually. Any experience-based study of healing, but especially one focused on energy and consciousness, can seem to go in all directions at once. We might be studying the chakras or energy movements in our bodies one day, and the anatomy of the neck on the next, but in reality, we are studying fragments of something a lot more mysterious than chakras, energy flows, and necks. When these subjects are studied as a hologram, anything we touch upon can draw us into a sense of wonder at that mysterious something which connects them.

So where do we begin? What are appropriate starting points? Probing with our consciousness into the human energy field, we find we are embedded in a multi-dimensional system that is at once within and without us, encompassing the entire diversity of elements that we humans can link with. Our flesh body and its senses connect us with all that we encounter as "external" to ourselves: the multifarious animal and plant species, land, air, water, and weather of the environing earth. Our consciousness carries us into the personal inner world of our emotions, energy movement, sexuality, beliefs, memory, altered states of consciousness, family, karma, love, society, personal history, evolution, thought, religion, spirituality. In our interconnection with others, we relate to the mysteries of culture, family, language, a sense of history. Beyond the confines of the human story, we may encounter the primal movement of spirit. In reality, any beginning point will do, for in the cosmos of human experience, everything is interconnected. This plays hell with any attempt to teach energywork in a straight-line fashion. And so, as students of energy healing, our task is to find ways of learning from whatever we experience.

Subtle energy practices are a means of taking part in processes that pertain to the whole person, as energy is the lowest common denominator of all our experience. These practices are a way of addressing themes and principles at work on every level of organization of life, on the vast human continuum of human experience, from disease and problems to awakening to life's possibilities, self-expression and creativity, to spiritual aspiration and union with the Divine.

Albert Einstein once said: "The state of mind which enables one to do work of this kind is akin to that of the religious worshiper or lover. The daily effort comes from no deliberate intention or program, but straight from the heart." He was talking about his own work when he wrote these words, but he described what I believe to be the best approach to energy healing as well. No matter how it might at times appear, rest assured, there is definitely structure and discipline associated with the experience-based study of the nature of consciousness and healing, but it will conform more to structures that exist in nature than to structures that our logical and cultural minds create.

I. Trusting the Authority of Your Own Experience

God Bless the Child Who's Got His Own

> Rich relations will give you
> a crust of bread and such.
> You can help yourself,
> but don't take too much.
> Papa may have
> and Mama may have,
> but God bless the child
> who's got his own.
> —Billie Holliday

In order to really grasp energy and healing work, it has to be done from the inside, in the laboratory of our own bodies and consciousness. There comes a point in the development of each of us where it is not enough to let Moses go to the mountain for us and come back and tell us what is what. It does us absolutely no good to know about other people's responses to healing and energy movement if we do not know our own. There are no books (including this one) that will replace authentic personal experience. There are teachers, of course, but if they are worth going to, it is because they respect and love what happens to individuals as they grow spiritually. They are more interested in encouraging us to have our own experience than in trying to get us to have a version of *their* experience.

For many of us growing up in the modern world, energywork will require a level of introspection that challenges beliefs that we have held to be true for as long as we can recall. Whether we've thought a lot about it or not at all, we each have acquired a perspective about the nature of life. The subjects we are going to explore in this book may not be stories or truths that most of us have ever heard before. The very absence of this information may become the source of doubt or skepticism. For that reason, learning about energy often involves learning about our own beliefs, the stories we tell ourselves in order to make sense of our worlds.

The process of learning anything new can force us to revise the stories we tell ourselves, and the belief structures that live within us, for these flavor our perceptions of the world and determine what we understand, accept and reject. This is what people often mean when they say we each create our own experience of the world. That concept becomes increasingly apparent as we work at the energetic level, where we are challenged to interpret our experiences without the usual reference points. When we go into the area of non-physical experience, energy and healing, we are venturing outside of areas about which there is a great deal of widespread consensus. And the further away we move from consensus, the greater the necessity that we get our own means of separating the wheat from the chaff. We learn to trust our ability to find out what is real. What is at stake here is one of the quietest but most important turning points in the growth of each of us: trusting the personal authority that comes from having our own experiences.

The quality of so much human experience is determined not by our own actions or by the actual nature of the external world but by the stories we're busy telling ourselves. For instance, the quality of the experience of camping in the forest will be very different for a person who believes the forest to be filled with danger than it will be for the person who believes that being in the forest brings them closer to spirit.

The study of energy, which involves non-physical experiences, can profoundly challenge our deepest beliefs about what is real. There can be shattering moments in this work, when realities we have up to now ignored (because they are too far out), or only paid lip service to (because we want so badly for them to be true), unexpectedly become palpable as never before. They are often just quick glimpses, but they point to a larger, more all-inclusive picture of what is real. When an authentic breakthrough of consciousness from a higher dimension takes place, old, rigid belief structures tend to swoon on the spot, like Aunt Pittypat in *Gone With the Wind*. You might spring into action like a Southern gentleman and bring those old belief structures a dose of smelling salts, prop them up and revive them, but when a new, larger reality announces itself with enough force, that is usually the end of them. Like Aunt Pittypat, their era has passed.

Apropos of our study of energy, and the skepticism which we often bring to it, Stanislav Grof once said that the first level of resistance to entering altered states of consciousness is physical, and the second level is *philosophical*. This is an interesting observation because it has to do with our beliefs about what is real, about what may and may not be in our personal world. Energywork specifically challenges the view that nothing exists beyond the physical. Our view of life changes when we acknowledge non-physical reality for the first time. The acknowledgment amounts to walking off the edge of our materialistic worldview. Leaping into the unknown, we soon discover a reality we didn't even imagine was there—and our lives are changed forever.

In workshops, we often hear the question, "Was that real, or did I just imagine it?" How we answer this kind of question for ourselves can ultimately influence what we experience at an energetic level. I often answer that question with another question, "Did it have a real effect on you?" Once, during a workshop in Munich, I showed a participant where the energy point at her shoulder was, using my middle finger about half an inch away from her physical shoulder. Energy was intense around us all because of the practices we had been doing.

When the energy point reacted, it sent a wave of energy up and down her body. There was an almost audible "snap!" She flinched and began crying. It didn't hurt, she said, but the sudden, tangible experience of something "not real" upset her deeply.

The phenomenon of our resistance is so important to address in energywork because that resistance can override every bit of subtle experience that would otherwise allow us to embrace this new reality. We often encounter a perfect example of this when we begin a meditation practice. We worry about the crossfire of internal messages we encounter when we turn our attention inward. Voices on continuous-loop tape recordings run nonstop in our minds, filling us with doubt or even fear. Informational viruses seem to lodge in our cells. Often, these viruses have come into our lives long ago, during the vulnerable period of childhood, for example, but even now they leave us vulnerable, with no experience of our own to fall back on. These might not be stories we are busy thinking actively to ourselves, but they are present as structures in our energy field, or a background program. They have a way of bouncing into our consciousness the moment we move into areas of experience not covered by prior knowledge.

Key Questions to Ask Yourself

Why do you believe what you believe? Upon what stories is your inner experience of the world based? Where, specifically, do your beliefs come from? Not just religious or philosophical beliefs, but beliefs about everything. Beliefs about who you are, where you came from, and where you are going. Beliefs about what is real and what isn't. Do your beliefs arrive in your DNA, hard-wired into your system? Are they codes, permanently chiseled into the bones of your personality? In order for the question "What do I believe?" to not simply call forward a list of personal articles of faith, it may need to be translated into a number of sub-questions like *"What is real for me? How do my beliefs function in my daily life? What is the carry-over from my beliefs into what I do?"*

Once you have articulated some of the beliefs you hold, it's time to ask yourself the question: *Are my beliefs really my own?* This is always a good question to ask because beliefs can come to us from so many sources. An entire, comprehensive package of belief structures has come to each of us by virtue of having been born into our particular family and culture. We have an identity determined by our "tribe," that includes stories about who I and "my people" are, who "they" are, your friends and enemies, where I came from and where I am going. Do I and "my people" come from Alpha Centauri or from the Milwaukee area?

Take a belief and trace it back as far as possible. Which parts of your belief structures came to you from your parents, from school, from your religious instruction? Contrast this with what you believe because it is part of your own experience, perhaps an area that distinguishes you as different from your tribe. This could be as mundane as your choice or cars or as fundamental as your religious or spiritual beliefs.

Which of your own firsthand, experientially-based beliefs have you acted on? Chances are, they have a lot of power. As an example, let me share with you an experience of my own: I will never forget the day I announced to my parents that I intended to join a religious order. The decision had been brewing for a long time, of course, but the instant I *said* it, a stunned silence filled the room. A palpable barrier—it was exactly like the Gardol Shield in the old toothpaste commercials—came between us. I didn't know I was doing it at the time, but with my announcement I had stepped through an invisible membrane around my particular tribe's consensual reality.

When a person begins to break out of tribal belief structures, disconnecting from its mindset and beliefs, it amounts to a significant rite of passage. You are no longer completely identical to your tribe and its mass mind, once you enter into the mysteries of having your own personal inner life, and especially when you begin to act on it. In this sense, growing the skills of a healer means leaving your tribe. You might return later, but your relationships will not be the same.

Are your beliefs progressive? That is to say, do they change and grow as you change and grow? This may be the best way to find out if a belief is truly your own, or one that you have accepted from an external source. One of the great problems associated with having other people's experiences (which is basically what we are doing when we accept uncritically an external belief structure) is that you have no means of progressing a belief which is not your own beyond a certain point. Trouble is, there are so many subtle inducements to do just that, even long after conquering some of our knee-jerk tendencies to try and be the nice boys and girls our parents wanted us to be.

If we are only copying someone else's beliefs or imitating their style—beyond the time it takes to absorb a lesson and make that lesson our own—it will come back to haunt us in the form of insecurity when it comes time to move beyond it. When it comes to our own belief system, we have to, as the golfer Ben Hogan put it, "dig it out of the ground" ourselves. For a long time most of us have to braille our way through a maze of authorities and received beliefs before we find out what we ourselves believe. But no matter how much doctrine we sop up, our spiritual development is driven by impulses which will take us toward our own truths and beliefs if we are patient and give them a chance.

This seems to come with the territory when it comes to learning energywork. Confronting and challenging our own beliefs is a critical part of being able to open ourselves to experience energetic realities. By now it should be abundantly clear that in order to make sense of our discussions about energy we need to find ways to actually *experience* it. Just knowing the theories of energywork or how other people respond to it isn't enough. We need to know it from the perspective of our own responses. The rhythm and dynamic of healing and spiritual growth are definitely not the same on paper as they are when we experience them in our own bodies and consciousnesses. We need a laboratory where we can sit down, probe the way we are organized energetically, and have experiences that will help to close the gap between theory and practice. In the following pages, you will find exercises for doing just that.

II. STRUCTURE AND DISCIPLINE OF EXPERIENTIAL EXERCISES

General Preparation for Energy Exercises

In offering the exercise guidelines you will find in this section, I ask that you take them seriously. The inner world which they open is potent, both in its capacity to heal and to confront, so these practices ought not to be done lightly. In most cases, an incorrectly done exercise will simply not do much at all. In other cases, where instructions about sequence of steps, length (in time) and frequency of the practice and direction of movement are not followed, some people will get momentarily "spaced out." Others will find unconscious material surfacing in ways that can be confusing or uncomfortable, especially for persons unused to working on themselves. As you venture into this exploration, be advised of the following, which I borrow from Robert Johnson's book *Inner Work*:

> You must understand that when you approach the unconscious you are dealing with one of the most powerful and autonomous forces in human experience. The techniques of inner work are intended to set in motion the great forces of the unconscious, but in a sense this is like taking the cap off a geyser: Things can get out of hand if you are not careful. If you fail to take this process seriously, or try to turn it into mere entertainment, you can hurt yourself.
>
> None of this should dissuade you from doing inner work. We are only observing a universal law: Anything that has great power for good can also be destructive if the power is mishandled. If we want to live intimately with the powerful forces of the inner world, we must also respect them.

And so I urge judicious use of this material, which comes out of many years of my own practice, and the experiences of my teachers, clients and workshop participants. Much of the material has been drawn from ancient world traditions as well. To do these traditions justice, I wish to promote a sense of the sacred in the responsible use of this knowledge.

There is an intentional design to each exercise. They are put together with a beginning, middle and end. They are constructed specifically to

- allow you to enter some area of experience;
- in some cases, create the opportunity for emotional, physical and mental release;
- draw in energy from higher dimensions of consciousness (this is what makes them *healing* exercises); then come back to normal body awareness and integrate what has been contacted during the exercise.

ENERGY EXERCISE GUIDELINES

1. **Find an appropriate time.** There might be certain times of
day that are better than others for doing energy exercise.
Experiment around until you find good times for you and your personal rhythms. Find times when you will not be disturbed. Tell
others with whom you live that you need this time to yourself.
Unplug the phone. *Know also that doing certain exercises just before
going to bed can keep you awake.*

2. **Allow time between exercises.** Unless otherwise recommended, allow a day or two between days when you do a specific
exercise. If you are doing two different exercises concurrently, simply do them on alternate days. Note that it takes about 36 hours
for the altered movement caused in the energy field by the exercise
to register at the level of bodily consciousness. This time period
allows for the grounding and integration of the energy you draw
into your body by doing the exercise.

3. **Be precise.** Check the subtle anatomy lessons in the second
Etheric Laboratory which talks about energy-active positions if you
are uncertain as to how to find a specific point or chakra. It is
important to get a good contact with them.

4. **Observe good body posture.** Unless otherwise indicated,
do these exercises sitting upright or even standing, but not lying
down. An erect, relaxed posture with the feet on the ground is generally most conducive to breathing easily and creating a good contact with the earth. In addition, a lying position is most people's
habitual sleeping position. Granted, this is a shift in consciousness,
but not the one we have in mind with the exercise!

5. **Breathing Pattern:** Unless otherwise indicated, the breathing pattern for these exercises is in through your nose and out
through your nose.

6. **No marathons.** Observe the time periods. They are important in all exercises, especially those in which there is a meditation
period or a "release phase." The reason for this is, again, the need
to ground and integrate what is drawn into your energy system
when you do the exercise. In addition, when an exercise is to last a
predetermined amount of time, it means there is a mechanism in
place for "coming back" from whatever you encounter in the exercise. This can be of great help in gaining the confidence necessary

for entering areas of consciousness which might otherwise be daunting.

7. **Do all the steps.** Be careful to observe and do each step of the instructions. If you do not understand an instruction it is better not to do the exercise at all, rather than doing it and doing it wrong. Simply drop the exercise that is giving you trouble and move on to an exercise that is clear to you.

8. **Keep a journal, either written or tape-recorded.**

9. **Honor the Context.** Finally, here is a request which we make to all our workshop participants, one which I also make to you. Please keep these exercises to yourself. They have come to you in the context of this book which prepared you to work with them. Unless you are willing and prepared to do the same for those with whom you would share this work, don't piecemeal it out.

Each of the exercises we work with can have very strong effects. If they are done regularly over a period of time, they will tend to draw you into what I call a "trajectory of effects," that will influence your personal self-healing process, and can be tracked on many levels. I'll be going into this in some more detail in the self-administered workshop portion of the book when I talk about the attributes of the etheric body. The only way to responsibly prescribe such an exercise to another person is to make certain you are familiar with how it affects you over a period of time.

Moving in the Etheric: Like Winding Up a Ball of Yarn

In my workshops I like to share the following story because its message illustrates the nature of the process you are about to undertake in the etheric, the medium in which we will be doing the main part of our energywork: When I was very young, my mother threw me out of the house once and told me not to come in until she said I could. It was a cold day in December, my birthday, and she was getting the house ready for the party. When I finally got to come back in, my friends and I—seven towheaded boys—entered, amazed, into a house full of multicolored webs. Rainbows of bright yarn streaked the air, the floor was slung with braided trails, leading from room to room, strung over and under each piece of furniture. Each kid got a strand and as we scrambled to wind up our yarn in a ball—we knew

there was going to be something cool at the other end—we reached
places where each of our strands were tangled up like spaghetti
Bolognese in everybody else's. We wiggled through colored clumps of
knots—I don't recall anyone getting mad and breaking his yarn—and
raced on, little pilgrims scurrying to Mecca, over sofas and around
piano legs. My mother deliberately made it hard to get untangled so
she could sit down for coffee and a smoke, and put her feet up. After
what seemed like hours, we arrived at the party favors tied to the end
of our yarn, and then promptly traded them off for someone else's.

Moving in the etheric has a lot in common with this yarn game
because when we really connect our awareness with the etheric and
allow it to move us, we will be led around many unexpected corners
on the way to our "destination." (One thing that the two activities do
not have in common is the fact that when you move your consciousness in the etheric you can't "scurry.") The ability to do subtle energy
exercises and to give intuitively guided energy treatments flows from
a set of basic skills which have to do with how we use our attention.
Attention, after all, is a focus of energy and consciousness; when we
develop our attention to a degree, it becomes a powerful tool. One
important etheric navigation skill is that of linking our attention or
awareness with energetic movement—let's say of a chakra—and
allowing ourselves to be drawn into that movement without totally
losing ourselves in that movement. Remember that it is the nature of
the etheric to draw our attention to deeper aspects of ourselves, so this
often means going places we had not intended to go. Therefore, it
takes a special kind of trust and letting go, which requires practice.

III. ETHERIC NAVIGATION

What follows is a little series of exercises which will help you school
your attention and use your awareness effectively in the etheric. This
will not only help you learn to navigate the etheric, and enliven it in
the process, but also help you to develop the ability to remain in a
state of relaxation over an extended period of time.

The task in this exercise series is to develop a way of focusing your
attention directly on the etheric, an important starting place for doing

conscious self-healing using the energy field. What is presented here is a series of steps for doing this, beginning with unplugging from the phenomena that usually have your attention, and then learning to move with the etheric, both intentionally and by letting the etheric move your awareness. The exercises will begin on the physical body, because that gives you your solidest point of reference. The process gets really interesting, however, when we use the points and streams and the chakras of the etheric as our beginning points. But let's take it step by step. Here is a way to start:

BASIC ETHERIC NAVIGATION EXERCISE # 1:
Learning to Trust the Etheric

Part 1: Mindfully Disconnecting From What Has Your Attention.

This sort of practice has a long history in a variety of forms. Buddhist practice incorporates very nuanced knowledge of the psychology of attachment and liberation from the ten thousand things that hold us in thrall. The Christian contemplative tradition teaches release of the mind from "the world." Such practices aim to bring our awareness into the present moment.

    1. **Sit quietly and notice where your attention is:** For example, your thoughts might be on work, on answering the phone which is ringing, or on places you would like to go for your summer vacation. Watch where your attention goes. Don't try to change it. Don't try to keep it from changing. Give this a couple of minutes. Just observe. Don't judge.

    2. Now **disconnect from this focus and draw your attention back to your body:** For instance, maybe your thoughts were a million miles away, thinking about something that happened in the past. Now shift your attention back to how your body is feeling, sitting in the chair, breathing softly. Simply focus on whatever you are experiencing in your body.

    3. Repeat the first two steps a number of times.

This simple-sounding step is probably the most important single exercise in this book. It sets the stage for all other self-healing and conscious-expansion exercises to come. This is a place to use creative visualization. Here are some suggestions:

- Imagine an electric cord plugged into the image or thought which has your attention. Now unplug from that image and pull the cord into your body.
- Imagine a rope tied with many knots around what has your attention. Now see the knot loosen, untie or slip apart. Pull the rope into your body.
- Imagine a tentacle like those of an octopus, with suction cups latched on to something. See the suction cups detach. Draw the tentacle back to you.

- Think of your attention as the way you send out your spirit and then "call your spirit back" to you from the errands it has been on. When you see where your attention and energy are invested, say, within yourself, "I call my spirit back." You have the authority and the power to do this.

NOTE: Like any other exercise or practice involving our energies and spirit, this takes practice and honesty and time. Do not naïvely assume that "pulling the plug" a few times in a visualization means that you have resolved a long-standing issue. In most cases, our spirits have been scattered to the four winds over a long period of time, and we call them back little by little, one grain at a time.

MINDFUL DISCONNECTION: When you are mindfully "unplugging" from what has your attention, it is a good time to use creative visualization.

Part 2: Letting the Etheric Move You

The inspiration for this exercise segment came to me during a workshop by Wayne Muller, who was at that moment teaching a concept found in all meditation practices which emphasize mindfulness: a thought or sensation will rise in our consciousness, then recede, only to be replaced by another, and then another. The meditator simply registers this without attachment. Classic forms of this type of practice include Vipassana and Zen meditation, which teach you to continually return to a primary focus, such as an image of the Buddha, or a flower, the tip of your nose, the sound of a bell, or some other focal point previously chosen.

Here, however, we become "nomadic" with this concept by applying mindfulness to what comes forward inside us, waiting for it to shift into something else, then applying mindfulness to that until it changes. And so on. Here is how you do it:

1. **Start on your body:** After getting quiet, pick a position on your body, for example, your right thumb. There is energy activity in your thumb and the idea is to link up with it.

2. **Pay attention:** At each point along the way, you are waiting in an open state of mind to see what happens all by itself. Try to register the precise moment when your attention is drawn to something else. This will happen.

Here's how: First, "hang out" with your right thumb; pay attention to it. Just notice. It doesn't have to be a certain way. There is no specific way that you are supposed to feel. You are not trying to make something happen, and you are not trying to prevent anything from happening. Keep your awareness loose.

"Loose" awareness means fuzzy focus, not deep concentration. You are not fixing your attention on your thumb. It is as if you are allowing the particles of your awareness to gather at your thumb, but you are not cementing them into place.

Let your awareness hover there, loose. If you do this your awareness will be drawn into the energy movement that is there at your thumb.

3. **Go with a shift:** When a shift in focus occurs, allow your attention to move with the shift. Go with it and use the next "station" as your new point of "loose focus." It may be a body part, a sensation, thought, image, memory, etc.

See if you can catch the moment when your attention is drawn to something else. If an owl flew in through the window, it would get your attention because the motion would catch your eye. It is the same thing here: the movement in the energy field will catch your attention.

Maybe you are drawn to your elbow, or your ear. When that happens, let your attention settle on the new point of focus and do the same thing all over again: allow your awareness to gather there and see if you can register the moment it shifts to something else. Maybe this time you are drawn to your neck. Same thing. Go with the shift with flexible attention. You might be drawn elsewhere in your body. You might be drawn back to where you started and you might go around and around in the same pattern for a while. Keep paying attention.

4. **Wait for the next shift and go with it:** There may come a moment when you are drawn to something which is not your physical body. Instead of a tension in your wrist or a sensation in your ribs, a thought or image, a feeling or a memory might come into the foreground. Treat it the same way. Pay attention. Allow your awareness to gather at it.

5. **Go with this process,** letting your mindfulness move to each new locality as you shift your awareness. After doing this a while, it may occur to you that you are following the threads of some interdimensional webwork. Play with the notion that, if you let it, your attention is being drawn to something. Like my mother's game of the yarn with the party favor tied to the end, the destination is not the piano leg or the door jam where we are momentarily led. Working in the etheric is like this. You trust. You let it take you. You go with it. You see where it leads. Get good at this by starting on the body, which is the densest part of the energy field. Starting on your body will help you stay grounded and present.

6. **Slowly disconnect from the exercise** by taking a deep breath, perhaps standing up and walking around to return to your normal state of consciousness.

Trust: An Important State of Being

Energy exercise and meditation will always involve trust. When fear can be released and trust allowed to enter in, expansion is possible into the personal and transpersonal unknown. This means expansion to the edge of your known world, beyond which is the "vastness out there." From there, we move into the extra-ordinary, beyond what is ordinary, beyond what we have put in order for ourselves, into mystery. Trust is the element of consciousness and intuition which allows that expansion.

Once I was meditating by myself and suddenly realized that Amalie, the three-year-old daughter of the family I shared a house with, had crawled into my lap. She put her arms around my neck, rested her head against my chest and fell asleep. I had never before been subjected to another person's trust in such an absolute and unqualified way. I also became unusually aware of being surrounded by a sense of strength and protection. I knew that in the presence of such unconditional trust, I was also trustworthy.

BASIC ETHERIC NAVIGATION EXERCISE #2:
Twenty-one Breaths into the Center

You have probably found that, once you get the hang of it, simply paying attention draws you into some interesting and surprising, perhaps powerful kinds of experiences. They are far from random. Now that you have some experience with moving in the energy field and allowing the energy movement to carry you, it's time to school your ability to move intentionally.

One time-honored way is to use your breathing, probably the most universal form of meditation. This kind of meditation is characterized by mindfulness, witnessing, registering what comes up in us all by itself. Linking attention with breath creates a non-violent way of finding out what is beneath the surface of your experience. It is a means of attending to what is given in the moment, as opposed to elbowing your way into yourself, digging around and trying to make things happen.

The purpose of the following exercise is to teach yourself to move in the etheric by using your breath, and in the process to create some important energetic communication within your system. You can do this exercise either standing up or sitting down. Here is how you do it:

EXERCISE STEPS:

1. **Tip of your nose:** Bring your awareness to the tip of your nose and breathe slowly and completely, without forcing any particular rhythm upon your breathing. Feel the movement of the air as it passes by the tip of your nose. Take three slow breaths like this.

2. **Tip of your nose > bridge of nose and back:** Start at the tip of your nose. As you breathe in, move with your attention backwards along the top of your nose and come to rest at the bridge of your nose (between your eyebrows). Linger there until you breathe out again, then travel with your attention back down your nose to the tip. Take three slow breaths like this.

Don't hurry.

3. **Bridge of your nose:** Breathe in and out with your awareness at the bridge of your nose. Three slow breaths.

4. **Bridge of your nose to center of your head and back again:** Move your awareness into the center of your head on the in-breath and back out to the bridge of your nose on the out-breath. Three slow breaths.

5. **Center of your head:** Breathe in and out with your awareness in the center of your head. Take three slow breaths.

6. **Center of your head to your belly and back again:** Starting in the center of your head, move your awareness downward in your body on your in-breath; move it into your belly *below your navel.* Stay there until you begin your out-breath, then move back up your body into the center of your head. You can move your awareness either inside your body (e.g. along the front of your spine) or on the skin surface on the front of your body. Three slow breaths.

7. **Belly:** Breathe in and out with your awareness in your belly, below your navel. Three slow breaths.

8. **Release phase:** Release your connection to your breathing and meditate for 10 minutes, allowing anything that "wants to" to come forward in your awareness.

9. **Conclusion:** Gradually re-establish contact with your body, slowly open your eyes and end the exercise.

Basic Etheric Navigation Exercise #3:
The Etheric Body-Stocking

In this exercise you'll be expanding your awareness of etheric energy and its activation. It will also teach you how to relax deeply for an extended period of time. This particular exercise is divided up into four parts. I recommend that you read through all four parts before starting the exercise. Then go back and follow the instructions precisely.

Part 1: FEET AND LEGS—*Etheric Stockings*

EXERCISE STEPS:

1. **Start with your toes:** Drop your awareness down to your toes—on both feet at the same time—and feel them (with your awareness).

2. **Up both legs:** Beginning at your toes, move with your attention slowly on the skin surface the length of both your feet and then up both legs at the same time until you reach the level of your groin on the front

and your buttocks on the back. (As you do this exercise, it may be helpful to imagine that you are slowly rolling a soft stocking up your leg, then back down.)

3. **Groin:** Feel your groin muscles on both sides.

4. **Back down both legs:** Slowly move back down both legs on the skin surface until you reach your toes.

5. **Disconnect:** Feel all of your toes for a moment, then disconnect your awareness from this part of the exercise.

NOTE: The best etheric contact is made when you move your awareness slowly along the skin surface.

ETHERIC STOCKINGS: Beginning at your toes, move with your attention slowly on the skin surface the length of both your feet and then up both legs at the same time. It might be helpful to imagine that you are slowly rolling a soft stocking up your leg, then back down.

Part 2: HANDS AND ARMS—Etheric Gloves

1. **Start with your fingertips:** Now bring your awareness to the fingertips of both your hands at the same time. Make a feeling contact (loose awareness) with them.

2. **Up both arms:** Move with your attention up both your arms to your shoulders.

3. **Shoulders:** Feel the energy movement at your shoulders and armpits.

4. **Back down both arms:** Move down both your arms until you reach the fingertips of both your hands.

5. **Disconnect:** Feel all of your fingertips for a moment, then disconnect your awareness from this part of the exercise.

USEFUL IMAGE: Imagine that you are slowly rolling long, elegant gloves up your arms, then back down.

ETHERIC GLOVES: Starting at your fingertips, move with your attention slowly on the skin surface the length of both your hands and arms. Here, you might try imagining that you are slowly rolling long, elegant gloves up your arms, then back down.

Part 3: TORSO

Front:

1. **Up the front of your body:** Bring your awareness now to your genitals and groin muscles on both sides of your body. Allow your feeling contact to deepen here for a moment.

2. **Collarbones and shoulders:** Now move with your awareness slowly up the front of your body to the level of your collarbones and shoulders. Take a moment to feel what you feel there.

3. **Back down the front of your body:** Move now with your awareness back down the front of your body until you reach your groin and genitals. Stay here momentarily, allowing your contact to deepen.

Back:

4. **Up the back of your body:** Disconnect from this position on the front of your body and move your awareness to the top of your hips. Include your sacrum (tailbone). From there, move slowly up your backside. *Try to feel the activity of energy in your spine.* Stop when you reach shoulder level. Again, take a moment to feel your shoulders.

5. **Shoulders:** Now move down the backside of your body, again paying attention to the energy activity in your spine, until you reach the top of the hips and the sacrum.

6. **Disconnect from the exercise:** After feeling this position for a moment, release your awareness from here.

A NOTE ON SPEED: Different impressions will come to you, depending on the speed you are travelling. You see many things while flying over a landscape in an airplane, but see a very different terrain if you backpack through the countryside, something different still if you crawl through it on your hands and knees. When you slow down a process, you can see and hear that process unfold. If you race your awareness too fast over the skin surface in an exercise,

> *"Do not hurry;*
> *do not rest."*
>
> —GOETHE

you will not get much out of the exercise. If you move too slowly, or "get your plow in too deep" you'll bog down and lose consciousness of what you are doing.

Part 4: NECK AND HEAD—Etheric Turtleneck

1. **Up outside of your throat and head:** Make loose awareness contact with the front of your throat.

2. Move your awareness around both sides of your throat to the back of your **neck** (medulla) at the same time.

3. Move upward on all sides of your head (the back of your head, jawbones, face, forehead) until you reach the crown of your head.

4. Rest at this position for a minute. Try to feel the activity of the energy just above the crown of your head.

5. Move from the crown of your head down all sides to the back of your neck (medulla).

6. From your medulla, move around both sides of your neck to the front of your throat.

USEFUL IMAGE: Imagine that you are slowly rolling up an extra-long turtleneck shirt collar, first up your neck, then up over your face and head on all sides, then back down.

TORSO AND HEAD: Move with your awareness slowly up the front of your body to the level of your collarbones and shoulders, then back down again. Follow this with the same kind of movement on the back of your torso. For your neck and head, imagine that you are slowly rolling up an extra-long turtleneck shirt collar, first up your neck, then up over your face and head on all sides, then back down.

IV. SENSORIUM

Here we go with an important class of exercises, namely the sensing exercises. The practical application of energywork, both in self-healing and in work with others, involves the ability to sense energy vibration which is of a higher frequency than what is normally perceived via the physical senses. Normally, we are attuned to physical vibration, while attunement to nonphysical frequencies is regarded as "extrasensory." But this is a misnomer because the range of our sensorium extends well beyond the physical range of vibration, so we really aren't going outside of it. As a result, "ESP" becomes "Extended Sensory Perception."

In this lesson, you will learn sensing exercises that will help your sensorium to link with higher rates of vibration. This enables us to both draw into consciousness useful impressions and information, and to track energetic processes as they unfold. As with the exercises for moving in the etheric, these will take practice, but they're worth it.

A Note About What's Normal

What is the "normal" range of the physical senses? Behavioral science speaks of "absolute thresholds" of sensation. Psychologist E. Galanter described the absolute thresholds of conscious sensory perception like this: if you are an "average" individual, and if you are standing on top of a mountain in pitch darkness on a totally clear night, you can see the flame of a single candle on top of another mountain at a distance of 30 miles; you can hear a watch's ticking from a distance of 20 feet in a silent room; you can detect the scent of a single drop of perfume in a three-room apartment; you can feel a bee's wing dropped on your cheek.

Once, while I was spending several days and nights in silence and meditation, the energy was very intense in the sanctuary where I spent most of my time. It got so I couldn't sleep because my senses were extremely heightened. On the third night, I was hearing the humming of the refrigerator in the kitchen at the extreme opposite end of the sprawling ranch house. The refrigerator sounded like an insect buzzing in my ear. Really distracting! What really bothered me, though, was smelling the apples that were inside the refrigerator.

SENSORIUM EXERCISE #1:
What Do You See, Really?

The purpose of this exercise is to develop your observational skills and to extend the range of your sense of sight, not so much in terms of distance, but in the range of vibration your eyes can detect. It is through your senses that you gather the experiences which to a high degree are authentically our own. Studies of such things as color perception, for example, reveal that the color is not in the object we are viewing. Our experience of color is made possible by the nature of our senses. In addition, we each bring to whatever sensory information we encounter a rich overlay of interpretation and meaning. Through our understanding of these phenomena we begin to more fully appreciate how very individual experience can be. This exercise is a simple way to examine the gap between what we think we see and what is actually surrounding us.

EXERCISE STEPS:

1. **Observation of flowers:** Place some flowers on a table in front of you and observe them, in detail. Take some time to reflect on their beauty and what that means to you. This moment of observing beauty is an important part of the exercise, so don't overlook or ignore it.

2. **Observation of room:** Now simply sit relaxed and use your eyes to observe the room, all details of it in the field of vision in front of you. Take about five minutes.

3. **Visualize room:** Close your eyes and visualize the same room and its details. Five minutes.

4. **Compare visualization with observation:** Open your eyes and see how your visualization matches up with your observation. Are there objects that are present in the room that were not present in your mental visualization? Did you "remember" objects in your visualization that perhaps were not in the actual room? Just take note of these.

5. **Meditation:** Close your eyes again and move your awareness to your Heart Chakra and try to feel its movement. Spend another five to ten minutes in meditation, allowing any images, thoughts or feelings that are there to come forward.

6. **End the exercise:** Slowly disconnect from the exercise.

This kind of observation exercise, like the one to follow, can be a wonderful prelude to meditation because it teaches you to be firmly rooted in the present moment. Like all practices that cultivate mindfulness, such exercises school the ability you have through your senses to simply pay attention without adding to, or taking away from, the phenomena that present themselves.

In the exercise that follows, you will again use the sense of sight, but this time you will use it in a subtler way. In the previous exercise, you were sharpening your observation skills on the physical objects in the room around us. This time you will teach your eyes to see into a broader range of the visible light spectrum, namely light-source colors. This enhanced ability will come in very handy when you set out to sense energy movement in and around your body.

SENSORIUM EXERCISE #2:
Sensing Light-Source Color

This is another exercise dedicated to extending your senses. The idea here is to attune to various parts of the light spectrum. For this exercise, you use a candle because you will be working with light-source colors, as opposed to chemically produced colors, such as what you would have from a color picture in a book.

For this exercise, you will need a candle and a dark room. Here are the steps:

1. **Candle flame:** Sit comfortably in front of a lit candle, placed at eye level, about eighteen inches in front of your eyes.

2. With your eyes open, focus your attention on the flame. Take some time to inspect all the various parts of the flame.

3. As you gaze at the flame you will notice, just outside the bright part of the flame, a gaseous sheath. It looks like a vapor around the colored part of the flame. Inspect that sheath and try to get a sense of how far it extends outward around the flame.

4. **Choose a color:** When your eyes have adjusted to looking into the flame, choose a color from the spectrum (red, orange, yellow, green, blue, indigo, or violet) and see if you can find it in the area around the flame. Stay with that color a minute or so.

5. **Try other colors:** Focus in the same way on other colors, giving yourself time to link with each color. Open not just your sight but all your senses to the color vibration. What differences do you notice between the colors you see in the flame? Which ones seem more distinct or fainter than the others?

6. **Visualization:** Now close your eyes. Visualize the flame and, again, inspect all the various parts of the flame with your eyes closed.

7. Attune to the same color again and stay with it for a good minute.

8. **End the exercise:** Open your eyes and look at the flame again. Just observe the flame for about a minute, then release this focus and end the exercise.

SENSORIUM EXERCISE #3:
Sensing External and Internal Sound

Now that you have spent some time "stretching" your sense of sight, here is a sensorium exercise which focuses on the sense of hearing. The idea here is to exercise your ability to link with sound, both external and internal. The purpose of this exercise is to stretch your sense of hearing so that it can detect higher rates of vibration. Don't skimp on step 7, as this is the point in the exercise where, with practice, you can begin to sense the sound of the etheric. Here is how to go about it:

EXERCISE STEPS:

1. Sit comfortably so that you can breathe easily.

2. **Heart chakra:** Bring your awareness to the middle of your upper chest and make a feeling contact with your Heart Chakra. Chakra contact works the same way as any other contact in the mindfulness exercises in the last section. Simply allow your attention to come into a loose focus in the area of the chakra and allow your awareness to be drawn into the energy movement of the chakra. It takes practice, but it is easier than you might think. Stay with this contact for about a minute.

3. **Throat chakra:** When you have established a good contact with your Heart Chakra, move your awareness to your Throat Chakra. You contact this chakra by bringing your awareness to the front of your throat, just below your Adam's apple. Let this contact build up for about a minute.

4. **Listening:** After you have established contact with the Throat Chakra and let it build for about a minute, disconnect from that connection and simply listen.

5. Listen to the sounds in the room immediately around you.

6. **Expansion:** Expand your listening to beyond the room you are in. Tune in to the sound of the area surrounding your house, the traffic on the street, birds and squirrels, the rain, the wind in the trees.

7. **Listen to your body:** Now draw your listening back to your body and listen into your body. Spend some time listening to:

- Your heartbeat,
- Your breathing,
- The blood pulsing through your veins and arteries.

8. **Meditation:** Disconnect your focus from these sounds and sit quietly, allowing whatever wants to come forward within you to do so. Give yourself a period of around ten minutes for this meditation period.

9. **Exit from the exercise:** Now return to your normal body awareness. Breathe deeply a few times before slowly opening your eyes and ending the exercise.

More Than One Way to Skin a Cat: A Message of Comfort to All Energy-Sensing Slugs

I used to hate energy-sensing exercises when I was in the early phases of learning energywork, mainly because everybody else in the group was (apparently) so good at it. They came up with so much information when they were sensing the energy field, while I was having to make do with very little evidence that anything was happening at all. It didn't help to be married to one of the world's all-time energy-sensing aces, either! It reminded me of a Peanuts cartoon in which Charlie Brown and Linus are lying on a hill, watching the clouds in the sky. Linus points up and describes what he sees: over here, St. Paul addressing the Corinthians, and over there, God the Father reaching down to Adam in Michelangelo's "Creation" on the ceiling of the Sistine Chapel, or some such. And on and on, each image more grandiose than the one before it. And Charlie Brown says, "All I see is a duckie and a horsie."

In truth, I was sensing *some*thing when I used my hands in another person's energy field: with one person I would have a momentary feeling of openness and space around them, the next would give me the impression that they were jazzed up, or sluggish, or flat, or emotional, light, or heavy. Actually, I was pretty pleased with my duckies

TIP: Sensing Hand (singular) vs. Healing Hands (plural) When you use your hands in healing, you are likely to be using both hands, and when you do that, automatically engaging the exchange of energy that moves between them. You might think of this as "healing mode." "Sensing mode" is different: many healers find that they are able to sense more easily if they use only one hand for sensing energy movement. Try this: put one hand in back of you while sensing; that is to say, take it out of the polarity arrangement. It will take some experimentation to determine which hand is your stronger sensing hand.

and horsies, until I began to compare myself with what I thought all these world champion clairvoyants around me were doing.

Not everybody will sense the same way. Some will develop their sight or hearing, both objective and subjective. My wife Ursula often hears the sound of energy contact when she is working on another person. Others will find that they sense best through their hands. In any case, it is a matter of learning to attune to the faster-moving energy which surrounds and penetrates the physical body.

Did I mention that all these exercises—especially the sensing exercises—need to be practiced? Hang in there! Here is a small grab bag of exercises for your hands:

SENSORIUM EXERCISE #4:
"Pantone Hands"

The purpose of this exercise is to explore the feel of various color vibrations with your hands. As with all of these energy exercises, be patient with yourself, go slow, and recognize the necessity for ongoing practice. Release yourself from the burden you might put on yourself to rise to certain expectations. Instead, just use this and other exercises in this series to develop your gradually increasing awareness of the different qualities of energy. Here is what you can do to work with this:

EXERCISE STEPS:
1. Spread out different colored sheets of paper in front of you. (Pantone color sheets work great. They can be found in paint stores and art supply stores.)
2. Close your eyes and use your sensing hand to feel the differences between the colors. At first, you are not specifically trying to determine which color you are sensing, but rather simply noting *differences*. Spend some time just sensing, then answer these questions:

- Does one colored sheet feel at all different from the other?
- Is there a difference in temperature?
- Does one emit a feeling of more, or less activity, crowdedness or spaciousness?
- Do you sense varying rhythms or sounds? (Not all people will.)

- Try Pantone #325 turquoise next to Pantone #122 reddish yellow. There is quite a large difference between these two, so they can give you an idea of what a large contrast in vibration feels like tactilely.
- Try a violet color or a light blue color next to an intense red or an active orange color.
- Try using the back of your hand to do the above.

With some practice, even an energy-sensing slug like I felt myself to be when I first started can come up with some good results with these little exercises. Actually, there is nothing particularly mysterious about this way of sensing color, since each color has a very individual vibrational frequency and our tactile senses can be trained to detect these variations.

Now that we have worked on extending our sense of sight, hearing and touch, let's finish off this lesson with a short sequence of sensing exercises that I use frequently in introductory workshops.

SENSORIUM EXERCISE #5: "Etheric Taffy-Pull"

The purpose of this exercise is to help you learn "first hand" about the different ways energy movement can feel when you sense it with your hands around the body of another person.

Etheric Taffy-Pull

Squeezing and Stretching the energy between your hands

1. To begin, rub your hands together to activate the energy of etheric around them.

2. With your hands loose and your palms facing each other, let your awareness gather in the space between your palms. It really helps if you don't "freeze" your hands into one position, but rather keep them "fluid," slightly in motion, as if you were gently massaging the energy around them.

3. Slowly move your hands further apart, then closer together. Feel the difference changing the distance between them makes.

4. Now feel what happens when you "squeeze" the space between your hands. Feel what happens when you "stretch" it apart.

After you have taken some time to do this and get a sense that there is definitely something to feel in this fluid medium of the etheric between your hands, here are some variations to try:

VARIATION #1: "Shearing": Here, you let one of your hands cut across the energy radiation of the other in a shearing motion.

Shearing: Let one of your hands cut across the energy radiation of the other in a shearing motion

VARIATION #2: "Cutting Through": With your eyes closed, have a friend use his or her hand to "cut through" the space between your hands while you are sensing. See if you can feel what happens when your partner does this.

VARIATION #3: "Use Other Materials": With your eyes closed, repeat Variation #2; this time have your partner use a solid object, maybe the back of a chair, a piece of paper, plastic or metal, running water. See what differences you notice when your partner creates various interferences like this in the energy field between your hands.

Cutting Through

Conclusion

Sensing skills are central to anything you will undertake with energy healing. For most of us, it takes time and patience to develop them. Even highly clairvoyant persons require time to learn to sort out the impressions they are taking in. The above exercises are rather universal in nature because they will get you started if you are a beginner, and they will serve as a means of honing your skills if you are already an expert.

I have become a believer in the incremental approach when it comes to building energy-sensing skills, or any other resource, for that matter. I'll tell you one of the ways I have found that out. Knowing that my old car is going to need to be replaced one of these days, I

began, about a year and a half ago, to slip a one-dollar bill into the
glove compartment of my car each time I started it. Every so often I
take out the accumulation and put it into a bank account. This pain-
less method of saving for a car has yielded $4500 in eighteen months.

Don't be afraid to practice your sensing skills. Opportunities
abound, even if you don't have a partner to formally experiment on.
Try sensing the energy around your dog or cat, or on your significant
other when they're not looking, if you're feeling sneaky. Try it on your
plants. They really don't mind; you might find they like it, and you
can file away new sensing experiences every day.

In Part I, you began your exploration of the etheric medium in
which we will be doing most of our energywork. By doing the exercises on etheric navigation and energy sensing, you have hopefully
established some familiarity and comfort with the etheric in general.
It pays to get oriented in this way, so that you will land on your feet
when you venture deeper into the energy system. Now let's turn our
sensing skills toward a few of the stable features of the subtle anatomy, beginning with some "energy-active" positions on the body
which we will be using again and again.

First Etheric Laboratory
EXERCISES AT A GLANCE

Etheric Navigation

Basic Etheric Navigation Exercise #1:
Learning to Trust the Etheric

Part 1: Mindfully Disconnecting From What Has Your Attention
1. Sit quietly and notice where your attention is
2. Disconnect from this focus and draw your attention back to your body

Part 2: Letting the Etheric Move You
1. Start on your body
2. Pay attention
3. Go with a shift
4. Wait for the next shift and go with it
5. Go with this process
6. Slowly disconnect from the exercise

Basic Etheric Navigation Exercise #2:
Twenty-one Breaths into the Center

Exercise Steps:
1. **Tip of your nose**
2. **Tip of your nose > bridge of nose and back**
3. **Bridge of your nose:** Three slow breaths
4. **Bridge of your nose to center of your head and back again:** Three slow breaths
5. **Center of your head:** Take three slow breaths
6. **Center of your head to your belly and back again:** Three slow breaths
7. **Belly:** Three slow breaths

8. **Release Phase:** Ten minutes
9. **Conclusion**

◦❧

BASIC ETHERIC NAVIGATION EXERCISE #3:
The Etheric Body-Stocking

Part 1: FEET AND LEGS—Etheric Stockings
EXERCISE STEPS:
1. Start with your toes
2. Up both legs
3. Groin
4. Back down both legs
5. Disconnect

Part 2: HANDS AND ARMS—Etheric Gloves
1. Start with your fingertips
2. Up both arms
4. Back down both arms
5. Disconnect

Part 3: TORSO
Front:
1. Up the front of your body
2. Collarbones and shoulders
3. Back down the front of your body

Back:
4. Up the back of your body
5. Shoulders
6. Disconnect from the exercise

Part 4: NECK AND HEAD—Etheric Turtleneck
1. Up outside of your throat and head
2. Around both sides of your throat to the back of your neck (medulla) at the same time
3. Crown of your head

4. Rest at this position for a minute. Try to feel the activity of the energy just above the crown of your head.

5. **From the crown of your head down all sides to the back of your neck (medulla)**

6. **From medulla, down around both sides of your neck to the front of your throat**

⤙❧

SENSORIUM EXERCISES

SENSORIUM EXERCISE #1:
What Do You See, Really?

EXERCISE STEPS:

1. **Observation of flowers**
2. **Observation of room**
3. **Visualize room**
4. **Compare visualization with observation**
5. **Meditation:** Ten minutes
6. **End the exercise**

⤙❧

SENSORIUM EXERCISE #2:
Sensing Light-Source Color

For this exercise, you will need a candle and a dark room.

1. **Candle flame**
2. With your eyes open, focus your attention on the flame. Take some time to inspect all the various parts of the flame.
3. As you gaze at the flame you will notice, just outside the bright part of the flame, a gaseous sheath. It looks like a vapor around the colored part of the flame. Inspect that sheath and try to get a sense of how far it extends outward around the flame.
4. **Choose a color**
5. **Try other colors**
6. **Visualization:** Now close your eyes. Visualize the flame and, again,

inspect all the various parts of the flame with your eyes closed.
7. **Attune to the same color again**
8. **End the exercise**

~&~

SENSORIUM EXERCISE #3:
Sensing External and Internal Sound

EXERCISE STEPS:
1. **Sit comfortably**
2. **Heart chakra**
3. **Throat chakra**
4. **Listening**
6. **Expansion**
7. **Listen to your body:** Spend some time listening to:
   • Your heartbeat,
   • Your breathing,
   • The blood pulsing through your veins and arteries.
8. **Meditation**
9. **Exit from the exercise**

SECOND ETHERIC LABORATORY
ENERGY-ACTIVE POSITIONS ON THE BODY

IN THIS ETHERIC LABORATORY, several pairs of "energy-active" positions in the etheric body will be introduced. These energy-active positions are among the stable features of the subtle anatomy. They interpenetrate with the physical and will become increasingly accessible to you with practice. Typically, these positions are named after the bodily landmarks they are associated with: i.e. shoulder points, pubic bone points, spleen. This is practical because it gives you an anatomical locus where you can start looking for the point. Besides, it gives us a common language for communicating with one another.

In this chapter, you will find instructions for locating and activating these energy-active points. You'll be pleased to know that the skills you've already developed in lessons one and two of Part I will be coming into play here. These have been selected because they are frequently used in subtle energy therapy and in basic energy exercises. You will appreciate this if you are doing healing work since they will have practical application for you.

There are some paired points (I'll explain this term soon) and a brief description of where they are located. Remember that any anatomical landmark is just an orientation point, a starting place for where to begin sensing them. The actual procedure is the same as the one we developed in Etheric Navigation Lesson #1 on linking our awareness with the etheric and letting the energy movement draw us in. Because of that, let's review the qualities that help that process, before we go on.

MINI-REVIEW: It is helpful to cultivate these qualities when linking awareness with the energy movement of the etheric:

- *Mindfulness:* Your attention is in the present.
- *Non-Judgmentalness*: You scare away experiences if you judge them.
- *Non-forcing approach:* You are not trying to make anything happen, and not trying to keep anything from happening.
- *Loose "fuzzy" focus:* This is different from concentration; do not fix your attention. It needs to be flexible in order to be drawn into the energy movement you are linking with.
- *Trust:* It is important to be as precise as possible, but even if you are not exactly on target in your search for an energy position, the presence of your attention will activate the area of the point or chakra. That activation will, in turn, draw your attention into its center, and that is the name of the game when it comes to linking your awareness with an energy-active position.

Polarity Positions: Anatomical Landmarks

Each of these pairs of energy-active points are stable features of the human energy system. The first five pairs are called "polarity positions" for a number of reasons. They resonate and interact with their counterpart on the opposite side of the body, so they play a strong role in energy balancing. The exchange between them also enlivens the midline of the body, facilitating a blend of activity at this meeting place, "where East meets West" in the body. It would be right to say that these positions also activate the poles and "midline" of our psyche. Even momentary balance between them helps to facilitate a shift in consciousness in the direction of that non-polarized state in which healing energy can be drawn into your system. (For a discussion of this phenomenon, see the Closing Talk: Progressive Healing: A New Look at Polarity in Healing, toward the end of the book.) The energy movement of these points can be palpated with light touch, or just off the body at the following anatomical positions:

POLARITY POSITIONS

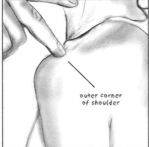

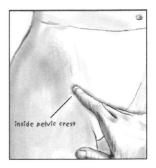

SIDE HEAD POINTS: These points are located two finger-breadths up from the tips of your ears on either side of your skull.

SHOULDER POINTS: You will find these points at the outer "corner" of your shoulder, where your collarbone and shoulder blade meet.

HIP POINTS: Look for the hip points just inside the curve of your pelvic crest.

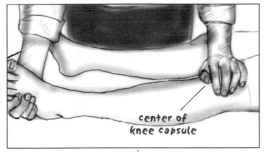

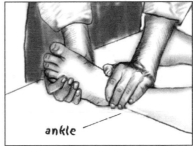

KNEE POINTS: The energy-active position at the knee is actually a minor chakra at the center of knee capsule. When activating this position with your hands, simply place your palms on the knee cap or on the inside surface of the knee joint.

ANKLES: To activate this energy position, simply place your hand over the top of the ankle. You can also place your hand over the ankle like a "saddle" with your thumb down one side of the ankle, and your fingers down the other side.

OTHER POSITIONS WE WILL USE

"Medulla": The back of the neck. When activating this position, you can simply place the palm of your hand on the back of your partner's neck, below the base of his skull.

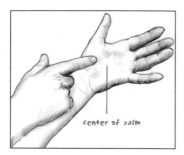

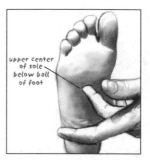

center of palm

upper center
of sole
below ball
of foot

HAND CHAKRAS: These minor chakras
are located in the center of your
palms.

FOOT CHAKRAS: The foot chakras can be
found in the upper center of soles of your
feet, below the balls of your feet.

Getting Acquainted with Polarity Positions

Spend a minute or so finding and sensing each of these points. If you
are using your hands on a partner, use a light touch on the skin surface,
or just off the skin. Try to come into the same "sensing mode" as you
used in the energy sensing exercises in the last chapter. If you are sensing these positions on yourself, use your awareness. Note which points
are easy to find and which are difficult. Some of these positions in the
etheric may already be so active that you can instantly locate them by
bringing your attention there. If that's not the case, the usual pattern
for sensing them is to move your awareness to the physical landmark
and allow it (your awareness) to be drawn into the energetic movement.
If you are in doubt as to whether you are really making contact with an
energy position, it may be a good idea to start your contact at the level
of the physical body—even touching the position with your fingertips
if you need to, and allowing the point to become active. Then remove
your finger and, while you still have a sensation in that area, move there
with just your awareness, without the help of your fingertips.

People vary greatly in how they experience these energetic points,
using words as diverse as aliveness, lightness, excitement, pulsation,
tingling, electric current, warmth to describe their sensations. That
said, it is important to guard against searching for something that
other people have reported; the best approach is to wait for your own
experience and trust it. Describe your energetic experience in your
own private way. As with all etheric work, practice will take you to a

place where you are secure in what you are experiencing. Believe me, you will know when it happens.

Once again, here are the steps:

PRACTICE WITH YOUR SHOULDER POINT

1. Move your awareness to the "corner" of your shoulder, where your collarbone and your shoulder blade come together. Go ahead and trace those bones with your finger, if you want.

2. Use the same "loose awareness" we practiced in Lesson #1, Part 1. Just locate the position with your awareness, then "hang out" there, not concentrating or fixing your attention.

3. Let the movement of energy draw your attention.

> *"The more you practice, the luckier you get."*
>
> BEN HOGAN

Elementary Polarity Protocol

In the following, you'll need to work with another person. For this, you might enlist the help of a friend or family member. Be sure to read this section carefully before you ask another person to help, so that you will be able to explain to them what helping you will involve. You may otherwise find that your helper is resistant or non-cooperative simply because they do not know what to expect. Remember, this may be a brand new kind of experience for them—and possibly for you, as well.

It is easiest to work with a massage table so that you can stand comfortably in an upright position, with your own energy flowing freely. If you don't have a table available, do your best to improvise. The floor can work fine, though it might not be as comfortable for you as you give the treatment. Spread out a blanket or two for padding and ask your partner if she would like a cushion under her knees and, perhaps, under her head. One thing I have used in a pinch is a small rubber raft on the dining room table. Whatever you use, recognize that your comfort and your partner's comfort are important and will have an effect on the outcome of the treatment.

The following instructions assume that your partner is lying down on her back, face toward the sky. Illustrations are provided to show you the hand positions.

> **PLEASE NOTE:** This is a very useful general treatment, quite safe to use with both sick and healthy persons. But I want to make two exceptions to this: Do not use this treatment on cancer patients with rapidly metastasizing tumors or on persons with severe schizophrenia. The reason is this: In both the person with active cancer and the person with schizophrenia, a part of the person's system has split-off from the whole (cancer cells, or a split-off aspect of the personality) and is operating independent of the general organization of whole person. Treatments like this, which make use of the polarity arrangement "right hand on the left side of the body, and left hand on the right side of the body" tend to invite a good deal of energy into a person's system. When the system is in as much disharmony as these conditions indicate, it is better to do things that will calm and harmonize the person, rather than activate their energy field, which can feed the renegade processes.

TREATMENT STEPS: HEAD TO FEET

1. **Occiput:** Seated or standing at your partner's head, looking down her body, cradle the back of her head (occiput) with both hands. (See Figure on page 59.) It can feel like you are gently scooping up her head in your hands. Feel the natural exchange of energy between your hands as it moves through your partner's head. This gentle influence will reinforce and help to balance the energetic exchange between the sides of the head. Give this a good minute in order to let the contact build up.

2. **Medulla/Forehead:** Connect your partner's medulla with her forehead. Here's how:

   a. With one hand, cradle the back of her neck (medulla) with either your entire hand just below the base of her skull (occiput), or use two middle fingers to contact the midline groove just below the occiput.

   b. With your other hand, place the palm of your hand on your partner's forehead. The palm of your hand is where the minor chakra of the hand is located. As the energy in your hands becomes more active, you'll feel this chakra opening. Just like in step 1, pay attention to what you feel between your hands. Each of these contacts will be slightly different. Let's see if you can sense that difference. Give this contact a bit of time to intensify.

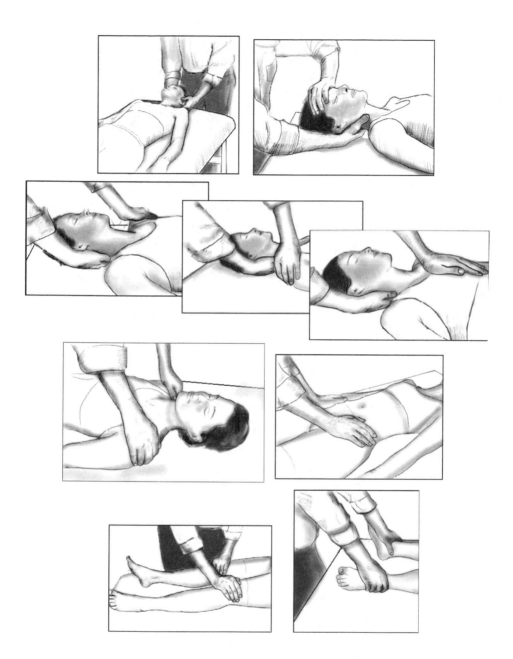

HEAD TO FEET: A simple way to initiate a polarity treatment is to begin by addressing, in turn, each pair of polarity positions. Here, the sequence is shown from head to feet. This is most commonly used, as the downward direction of movement tends to calm the energy system, while working from the feet to the head has a more activating effect."

How Do You Know When You Have Made an Energetic Connection?

First, it is good if you can simply trust that there is already a natural exchange of energy between your hands and that this exchange will happen all by itself when you lay your hands on another person, especially at the polarity positions in this treatment. Your sense of energetic connection can begin immediately, the moment you lay your hands on your partner, or it can set in gradually as the healing session progresses. The sensing skills you worked with in "Sensorium" will help you to become familiar and comfortable with this phenomenon. When I lay my hands on another person at energy-active positions, what I typically do is this: first, I pay attention to what is going on under my hands. Is there a pulsation or a vibration of some kind? If so, is there a rhythm to it? Once I have checked in to what's happening, I wait for a change. One dynamic that I encounter frequently is when one side is active and the other is not. As my partner's energy system responds to my touch, however, it is not uncommon for the inactive side to begin to activate with a weak, irregular pulse, and then come into rhythm with the other side.

Another way you know that you have made an energetic connection is by observing your partner. Does she show signs of progressive relaxation as you move into the treatment? Does she become quieter? Are her eyeballs moving back and forth under her eyelids? Do her breathing patterns change? The big tip-off is when your partner spontaneously takes a deep breath and lets it out. This tells you that her respiratory diaphragm is relaxing, so she can breathe more deeply. It also tells you that the energetic activity in the upper and lower parts of her body are joining.

3. **Medulla/shoulders/heart chakra:** Now, keeping one hand under your partner's neck, place the palm of your other hand (your Hand Chakra) in turn on your partner's left shoulder, right shoulder, and then on the Heart Chakra. (When placing your hand on your partner's upper chest in the proximity of the breasts, especially with women who are receiving the treatment, use your common sense. You may choose to leave this step out, or contact this energy movement just off your partner's body.) Give each of these combinations up to a minute. Trust the connection

to produce new activation, even if you don't feel everything that is going on.

4. **Shoulders:** After you have created the connections described in the first three steps, move around to the side of your partner. Stand or sit so that you are looking up your partner's body. *Place your right hand on her left shoulder and your left hand on her right shoulder.* Remember, this contact uses the center of your palm because that is where the hand chakras are active. Place it over the energy-active position we call the shoulder point. Check the illustration. You are allowing these two positions to interact. Let this contact build. This time, the energy movement is strengthened across the top of her body.

5. **Hips:** Release this contact and move to the hip points. Place the palm of your right hand on her left hip point, and your left palm on her right hip point. See the illustration for the recommended hand position.

6. **Knees:** Place your hands on both your partner's knees, right hand on her left knee and your left hand on her right knee.

7. **Ankles:** Repeat with both ankles.

BUILDING THE BIG POLARITY CIRCULATION

What we are going to do here is combine these positions in a way that enhances the energetic communication, not only between the right and left sides of your partner's body, but also between the upper and lower parts. This is the first energy treatment I ever learned, and I still use it, or parts of it, every day in my practice. It not only connects the energetic poles of your partner's body, but it also follows the dominant direction of flow of etheric energy up and down her body. We'll go into more depth about that flow in the next chapter.

ASCENDING AND DESCENDING LINES OF ENERGY FLOW IN THE ELEMENTARY POLARITY TREATMENT: In this treatment, you not only connect the energetic poles of your partner's body, but it also follows the dominant direction of flow of etheric energy up and down your partner's body.

ASCENDING SEQUENCE

As the giver of the treatment, you are standing next to your part-ner's right foot (see illustration).

1. **Left foot chakra/left ankle:** Place the palm of your right hand on your partner's Left Foot Chakra. Place your left hand over her left ankle with your thumb on the inside of the ankle and your fingers down the outside. Your left palm is riding like a saddle on your partner's ankle. Allow that contact to build a moment.

2. **Left foot chakra/left knee:** With your right hand still on the Left Foot Chakra, now place your left hand on your partner's left knee. You are extending the area of energetic exchange between your hands.

3. **Left knee/left hip point:** After a moment, pick up both hands and place them on your partner's left hip point and left knee.

4. **Ascending crossover position: left hip point/right shoulder point:** When that combination has had a bit of time to respond, now pick up both hands again and place your right hand on your partner's left hip point, and your left hand on her right shoulder point. This is an important position because the ener-getic exchange passes through the solar plexus area. It is the first time we have connected both the right and the left sides and the upper and lower body. Allow this contact to build for a good minute.

5. **Left hip point/right hand:** From there, simply keep your right hand on your partner's hip point and place your left palm on her right palm. If her hand is turned downward, toward the table, just sneak a couple of fingertips under her hand and contact her Hand Chakra like that. Give this contact a good minute.

6. **Right hand chakra/left knee:** Keeping your left hand (or fingers) in contact with her Right Hand Chakra, move your right hand to her left knee. Allow time for this contact to deepen.

7. **Right hand/left foot:** With your left hand still on her right hand, complete this first circulation by placing your right hand on her Left Foot Chakra. You have reached the "destination" for the ascending line of the polarity circulation. After spending a good minute with this position, release the contact.

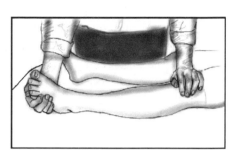
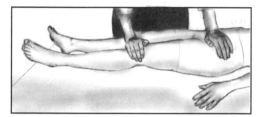
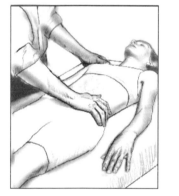
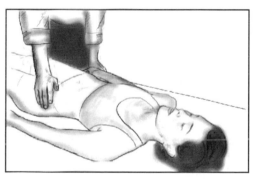
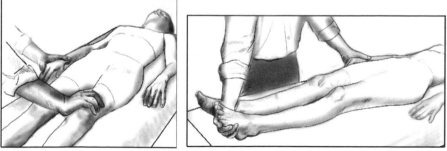

POLARITY TREATMENT STEPS (ASCENDING SEQUENCE): This sequence addresses the major etheric energy flow which moves up the front of the body.

Have you noticed that this has something in common with using jumper cables on your car's battery? One major difference is that on your car you connect the positive of one battery with the positive pole of the other, and negative with negative. Here, in our basic polarity treatment, when we put our right hand on the left side of the body, we are connecting positive charges with negative. The right side of the body has a positive charge—that means that the strength of energy activity on this side moves outward, away from the body—while the left side's strong movement is inward, toward the body. In polarity-style treatments, we try to make use of this energetic give and take in the circuitry of our bodies wherever we can do it conveniently.

DESCENDING SEQUENCE

1. **Left hand/left shoulder point:** Now come around your partner and stand by her left hand. Take her left hand in your left hand in a handshake position, palm to palm. Place your right hand over her shoulder point. Remember that this contact uses your Hand Chakra. Let this contact build up before moving to the next position.

2. **Descending crossover position: right shoulder point/left hip point:** Keep your right hand on her left shoulder point, reach across her body and place your left hand on her right hip point. Stay with this contact about a minute.

3. **Left hand chakra/right knee:** Release both hands and put your hand on her Left Hand Chakra, your left hand on her right knee. Allow one minute here to let the contact build.

4. **Left hand/right foot:** Keep your right hand where it is and move your left hand down to her right foot, completing the second circulation. Again, give this contact a good minute.

5. **End the treatment:** After giving this connection some time, release it and give your partner some time to feel the effects, then slowly come back to her normal state and slowly get up.

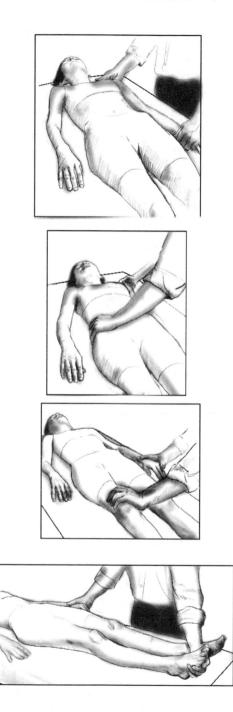

POLARITY TREATMENT STEPS (DESCENDING SEQUENCE): This sequence addresses the major etheric energy flow which moves down the front of the body.

The only difficult thing about this treatment is remembering the steps, but with a bit of practice the pattern becomes obvious. You will begin to relax with it as soon as you don't have to consult your notes for every move.

The benefits of this style of treatment is that it allows energetic exchange between the poles in our systems. In that exchange, many a one-sided holding condition can be addressed. A good, general treatment, this can be used with anyone. If a person is ill or wounded, their healing is accelerated when their system is energetically balanced. With the exceptions I mentioned at the beginning, you can use this treatment as soon as you feel confident with it.

Unwanted Energy Transfer and the Myth of "Negative Energy"

In workshops I ask students to share with one another what they experience during treatments, both as the giver and the receiver of the treatment. In a recent workshop, a woman described how she got a headache the second she laid her hands on her partner. As the treatment progressed, the headache gave way to sadness and she did at least half the session with tears rolling down her face. Her partner reported that she, too, had a splitting headache when she lay down on the table, but in the relaxation that came from the polarity treatment she was receiving, the sharp edges of her pain softened and she began to feel the sorrow that lay behind it. She had come to the workshop from the hospital where her father was slowly dying and she felt powerless to help him. Interestingly, the woman who gave the treatment said that as soon as the treatment was over, the headache and sadness were gone, as if they had never been.

Another time, I remember a workshop participant leaping up off the table and screaming at her partner that she didn't want his "angry vibes." When I asked her partner about it, a young man of twenty-two, it turned out that he was in personal turmoil, fuming over a situation at work that he felt was beyond his control, and he was very busy inside himself with this conflict with his boss. As it turned out, the woman who was to receive the treatment also admitted to having a good deal of anger in her life, in particular at her boyfriend, who couldn't keep a job.

These two situations have a lot in common. In the first case, the woman giving the treatment clearly felt in her body things that were going on in her partner's body. She was able to track very accurately the shift in her partner from headache to sadness to tears. On reflection, she was able to see that the headache and sadness she was feeling were not "her" headache and sadness. In the second example, the anger in one partner found a resonance with the anger in the other, and it seemed to short-circuit the treatment.

Two of the questions most frequently asked on the subject of energy healing are: "How do I, when I am giving a treatment, keep from picking up my partner's 'negative energy?'" and "Isn't it true that if I am depressed, angry or otherwise particularly negative when I give a treatment, I can actually do harm?" I see these questions as two versions of the same basic question because they both have to do with possible harmful transference of energy between you and the person you treat. These are important questions, and they ought to be asked.

We will never get away from the transfer of energy between us. Our energy fields interact constantly, though we are unaware of it most of the time. When we become involved with giving and getting treatments, we suddenly become aware of at least part of this interaction. One of the paradoxes of energy healing is that, on the one hand, in the process of sensing and treating another person, we are doing things which cause us to merge, or blend, with our partner, and on the other hand, we need to have good boundaries to protect both of us from any harmful exchange which might occur. How can we reconcile this?

First, I would like to address one of the assumptions that these questions make about how energy works. I believe the term "negative energy" arises from a mistaken notion about the nature of energy. In reality, energy is neutral, neither "good" nor "bad." Like the electricity that lights the bulb in my lamp, it can have a positive or negative *charge,* and it takes both in order to light the lamp, but this has nothing to do with value judgments.

Typically, what we mean when we talk about "negative energy" is energy that is stuck in an emotional pattern like fear, anger or depression. It is helpful to think of a pool of standing water that stagnates, but freshens when it is allowed to flow again and join the rushing stream. Then perhaps it evaporates and joins clouds and eventually falls to earth once again, maybe this time raining down on crops that nurture us. The water goes through many cycles of change, but remains water. It is much the same with energy.

In energy healing, we work with practices that bring about the movement and transformation of energy. This involves release of what has been held and, as healing progresses, the eventual clearance of the pattern itself. Like the water that freshens and becomes vital again once it rejoins its joyous natural cycle, the energy that flows through our bodies and psyches also goes through many transformations when it becomes unstuck and is allowed to move in its natural way.

Having said all this, we still have in front of us the question: "What can we do about preventing unwanted transfers between ourselves and those we give treatments to?" I believe we need a long-term strategy and an immediate one.

The long-term strategy is the ongoing work you do on your own healing. Anyone who is active with energy healing learns, sooner or later, that this issue of transfer is one of the reasons why it's important for him to work on himself. If you have unconscious, but highly charged, unhealed emotional issues in your life, they can really get in the way when you are trying to work on another person. The workshop partners whose treatment was derailed because of the anger which they activated in each other is a good example. Unresolved issues such as these literally act like a magnet for similar issues and energies which your treatment partner might have, tucked away within him. The good news is that as you resolve these issues within yourself, they lose their magnetic pull, and you will find that you can work with people with all kinds of emotional problems without being affected.

This is not to say that you need to be perfect, or "completely healed," in order to give energy healing treatments. If that were the case, nobody would be giving treatments. Still, it is important to understand this dynamic.

The more immediate strategy has to do with how you orient yourself when you give a treatment. You need to be able to sort out what is coming from your partner and what is coming from you, and align yourself with what gives you strength and clarity.

Obviously, you know who is who when you have your eyes open, but when you begin to blend your energy field with the person you are working on, all kinds of images, sensations and impressions begin to flow between you and your partner. This can be confusing if you don't have a means of discerning where these impressions are coming from, whether they are images coming from you or out of the other person's energy field. Here is a simple, but effective tip:

When you give a massage or energy treatment, instead of making contact with your partner as the very first thing you do, try *disconnecting* from your partner first. Before touching your partner, pull back into yourself and take a "snapshot" of yourself. Ask yourself:

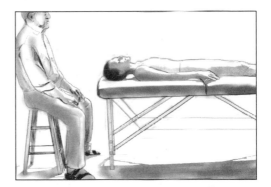

- How does my body feel? Are there areas of pain, restriction, discomfort?
- What is going on in my energy system?
- What is happening in me emotionally? Am I calm, centered, or upset? Am I aligned and focused, open to receive guidance?
- What are my attitudes and intentions at this moment?

When you give a massage or energy treatment, instead of making contact with your partner as the very first thing you do, try *disconnecting* from your partner first.

Just a snapshot is all you need. This will give you a basis for distinguishing between your own projections, on the one hand, and images which may come to you as helpful information for working with your partner, on the other, when you finally make contact with your partner. When you shift your awareness in this way, you are creating a semi-permeable boundary that will serve both you and your partner.

Once you have disconnected from your partner, the other important piece of this preparation for a treatment is your attunement to higher consciousness or a higher intelligence. Remember that energy follows your intention. This is the time when many practitioners pray for a blessing and guidance for this healing session. While one person might link with Light or Christ, another might call on his or her guides or angels, or those of the person about to receive the treatment, to be present. Or, you might simply get in touch with your best, most healing intentions toward the person you are about to work on. Whatever your orientation, it is important to shift your awareness to what you consider to be a source of healing.

What about giving energy treatments at times when you are not at your best? Can you do harm? While you obviously don't give treatments if you are on an out-of-control emotional binge, any more than you would work on someone if you had a contagious disease, you can still give very effective treatments even when you are down, or moody, or in a "negative space." The reason why this is so—and I've experienced this many, many times—is that if you can subordinate your ego, open yourself to a higher power and open in compassion for the person you are working with, and work within real energy principles, such as the polarity principle, you will create a situation that not only works in a healing way on your partner, but also on you. If you can't do those things, then obviously it is not time to do a healing session. Ultimately, you need to be the judge of that.

The healing energy you direct to your partner moves through your system first. Many times I have gone into a treatment feeling lousy, and come out feeling great, and my partner feels great, too. And it has nothing to do with "ripping off" your partner's energy. It is a mutual process. You and your partner blend and form a single energetic unit which is subject to the movement of healing energy. You can tap into a process that is much bigger than you.

It has consistently been my experience that these simple practices of first disconnecting from the person I am about to work with and attending to my inner orientation as I go along, together with the ongoing work I do on myself, give me confidence that allows me to open to my partner without fear. On the rare occasions when I do a session with someone who makes me feel uncomfortable or defensive, I take the position that this encounter has alerted me to something in myself that needed attention, so I have gained from the experience. In those few cases, I have referred these persons to a practitioner who I felt would be better able to work with them. If you are going to be involved with healing work, don't fall into the trap of trying to be all things to all people. One thing is for sure, though: the more you develop your skills and qualities as a healer, the more you will draw to you individuals who need exactly what you have to offer, and the more your sessions will take place in an atmosphere of love and openness. You will come through even the strangest and most challenging sessions shining like a new dime.

THE ELEMENTARY POLARITY
PROTOCOL AT A GLANCE

TREATMENT STEPS:
1. Occiput
2. Medulla/Forehead
3. Medulla/Shoulders/Heart chakra
4. Shoulders
5. Hips
6. Knees
7. Ankles

Building the Big Polarity Circulation

Ascending Sequence: As the giver of the treatment, you are standing next to your partner's right foot (see illustration).
1. **Left foot chakra/Left ankle**
2. **Left foot chakra/Left knee**
3. **Left knee/Left hip point**
4. **Ascending Crossover Position: Left hip point/Right shoulder point**
5. **Left hip point/Right hand**
6. **Right hand chakra/Left knee**
7. **Right hand/Left foot**

Descending Sequence: As the giver of the treatment, you are standing next to your partner's left hand (see illustration).
1. **Left hand/Left shoulder point**
2. **Descending Crossover Position: Right shoulder point/Left hip point**
3. **Left hand chakra/Right knee**
4. **Left hand/Right foot**
5. **End the treatment**

THIRD ETHERIC LABORATORY

THE ENERGY KIVA: CREATING AN ENERGETIC HEALING ENVIRONMENT

"The highest responsibility the
therapist has is to protect the spirit, the sense of hope and the life
force."

—RON KURTZ

Parasympathetic Shift: Coming Out of Defense Physiology

DURING AN ENERGYWORK session it is not unusual for a person to find themselves slipping into a kind of waking dreamstate, which is sometimes known as "journeying." This is a phenomenon most of us are familiar with. It is akin to daydreaming, in which we might relive a time from the past, imagining ourselves going through an old experience of pleasure or grief. Or we might even imagine ourselves travelling off in our minds to encounter new people or places that are entirely new to us. It is a state of mind in which insights can arise and it seems to be part of healing and inner growth. When the stage is set, journeying is an altogether natural event and will happen spontaneously. Some healing traditions say that we will fall ill if we lose our ability to move into and out of these dreamlike states. One of the most helpful things we can do as healers is to provide our treatment partners with an energetic environment where they can freely journey in this way, then come fully back into the present and explore what their journeys mean in terms of their everyday lives.

An example might be a stressed-out executive who comes into a deep state of relaxation during a massage or healing session and in the process imagines, to his surprise, that he is transported to a cool mountain lake. He finds himself swimming in its pure waters, naked and free. Following the session he might discuss this journey in terms of what he needs in his life—to rid himself of unnecessary pressures. He might reflect on the path he has taken, perhaps revealing that in his workaday life he is having to take on a role that is not really using his greatest potentials or may be in conflict with his true nature. This alone might be a major source of his stress.

The executive in the above example may have regarded the everyday stress that he feels as his "norm." To shift from this norm into a state of deep relaxation where he can freely journey, and then return to a state where he feels very present and grounded, is a liberating and healing discovery for him.

If we are to facilitate another person's shift into another state of consciousness, such as in the above example, we will need to enlist the cooperation of the body, the nervous system and the unconscious. This consists of more than verbally assuring your partners that they are now safe to let down their guard and enter an expanded state of consciousness. But to fully understand the importance of why it is so important to create an environment where all this can happen we need to be aware of what keeps it from happening in everyday life.

As Stan Grof said, the first two levels of resistance to entering altered states of awareness are physical and philosophical. Earlier chapters have dealt with the philosophical aspect. Let's look now at the physiological side, in particular the role played by the autonomic nervous system—that part of our nervous system that regulates automatic physiological functions which lie generally, though not exclusively, outside our voluntary control. There are two aspects of this system: the sympathetic nervous system, which is the mechanism for the "fight, flight or freezing" response, and the parasympathetic nervous system, which enables us to return to normal function after an episode of excitement or danger. These two sides of the autonomic nervous system operate in tandem to regulate involuntary functions such as respiration, body temperature, circulation and digestion, as well as hormonal activity. Alongside its regulation of specific areas of physiologic functioning, the autonomic nervous system also figures mightily in our ability to shift the focus of our awareness from outward matters, such as completing a task at work, to inner work, such as meditating on what you should do with your life.

One of the most dramatic differences between the sympathetic and the parasympathetic is adrenal function, that is, the secretion of hormones such as epinephrine and norepinephrine, which flow through the blood stream in response to muscle tension, or relaxation and stress that we experience mentally. If you are walking through the jungle and look up to see a tiger leaping at you through the air, roaring, claws extended, fangs glistening, your sympathetic nervous system will respond in a split second, long before you would be able to think up a response. Your pituitary gland, located in the middle of your head, and your adrenal glands, situated on top of your kidneys, trigger a whole array of supercharged reactions in your body and mind: your pupils dilate to dime size while the field of your vision narrows, your muscle tone increases while your organs of digestion stop, your respiration accelerates, heart rate and blood pressure increase along with the blood supply to the large muscles in your body which you would use for fighting and/or running away. Let's call all of these responses "defense physiology." In the split second after you see the tiger flying through the air at you, defense physiology responds to get you as ready as possible to do battle or escape—fight or flight.

Chances are, you choose the second option. You run like hell and somehow escape. Upon settling back down in the safety of your home, it is the parasympathetic nervous system that begins to normalize your heart rate; your blood pressure drops, your adrenaline output at last is slowed. Food might begin to look good again. Or your digestive organs might overreact, causing vomiting, diarrhea, or frequent urination. By and by, however, relaxation and rest once again become possible. Of course, when you tell your friends about your narrow escape from the man-eating tiger, your sympathetic nervous system kicks in again, along with all the various effects in a somewhat milder version of the original experience. This time, however, the responses of your autonomic nervous system are not triggered by the tiger, but rather by your *memory* of the tiger.

The autonomic nervous system does not know the difference between real and remembered or imagined events. This explains why our bodies tense up and we have all the sensations of adrenaline rushing through our systems when we watch a frightening movie or remember a frightening experience from the past. It also explains why we become stressed at times when there is no real physical threat, as when we are facing a pressured deadline or we become angry at our boss at work.

When our sympathetic nervous system is caught up in the heightened psychophysiological (mind-body) state of defense physiology, specific priorities set in, all of them focused on our *survival*. Healing and expansion of consciousness are not among them. The normal functions of healing are put on hold when the sympathetic nervous system is on red alert; there is no unnecessary expansion of consciousness when the organism is tightly focused on survival. On the contrary, all our senses and muscular responses are focused on the threat we are facing and actions we can take to prevent harm to ourselves. The well-known upshot of this is that those of us who may have experienced constant threats as children, or some traumatizing event, may grow up to live in a state of hypervigilance and remain in this same state of defensiveness at all times. Instead of the rare, intense activation of the sympathetic nervous system, which helps us momentarily if we encounter real danger, a low- or medium-intensity version of this becomes a permanent state which we perceive as "normal."

Though most of us don't live in fear of imminent animal attack, we do need, to a greater or lesser degree, to come out of a state of hypervigilance or psychophysiological defensiveness in order to heal and grow consciously. This is why for many people the first step in a healing process is to teach the body and mind to make what I call a "parasympathetic shift," that is, a shift out of the defense physiology characterized by the dominant activity of the sympathetic nervous system.

One of the tragedies of child abuse is that it places a strong imprint on a young person who is overwhelmed by situations which he or she has no means of dealing with. A similar situation may arise for a person who is in a violent car wreck; most people cannot experience such a thing consciously. Our first reflex is to blank it out completely. The resulting trauma comes about when consciousness exits from the body (a version of the flight part of defense physiology). This kind of wound can take a long time to heal. Memories of traumatic events can arise later in life, and this "replay" can keep the autonomic nervous system "stuck" in fight-or-flight mode, unable to shift. Often these memories are stored in the tissues of the body. When consciousness re-enters areas where that memory is stored, the memory—and possibly the original fight or flight response—can be re-activated. In extreme cases, unresolved trauma can render a person almost incapable of entering into a state of rest and healing. This ability to shift into a healing mode of consciousness often needs healing as much as do the actual wounds a person has sustained.

Energy healing can awaken memories stored in the body. Remember that the etheric layer of the energy field, which is inter-woven with the physical body, is a medium for memory, and it is the nature of the etheric to bring unresolved and unhealed aspects of our-selves to the surface of our conscious so we can attend to them. One of the challenges for you in your role as a healer is to create for your partner a means of shifting out of the hypervigilant or traumatized state, clearing a space for consciousness and healing energy to enter areas that were injured, either physically or emotionally, and do it *without* triggering an escape response. By "escape response" I mean our natural tendency to deny or try to push away truths that are painful to us. Creating the nurturing, healing environment where all this can occur requires that we build a relationship of safety and trust which consists of much more than encouraging words. I like to think of this as "building an energy kiva."

Building the Energy Kiva

I first saw kivas, deep concave enclosures dug into the earth, at Chaco Canyon in New Mexico, where ancient Anasazi ruins have been excavated. Some kivas served as meeting places and kiosks, or markets, while others still are used only for initiatory and ceremonial purposes. When I first saw a ceremonial kiva, I thought, "That is exactly what energy healing is supposed to do: provide treatment partners with a 'kiva' (an energetic one) for their healing processes!"

The idea is to create a ceremonial enclosure, a protected, sanctified environment dedicated to a sacred activity, like initiation and healing. Rennard Strickland, author of *Tonto's Revenge: Reflections on American Indian Culture and Policy*, reinforces this idea: "Kivas, with their myth-ic wall murals, became cosmological vessels wherein past, present, and future osmotically combined, revitalizing the ceremonial cycle that harmonized the world."

Ideally, all energy exercises and treatments ought to create an "energy kiva." Obviously, this doesn't mean you need to go out in the backyard and dig a hole in which to do treatments. Still, we need to bring the principle of enclosure and containment of sacred processes—so vivid in the traditional ceremonial kiva—into the energetic healing environment in which we work. Like its earthen counterpart, the energy kiva is an enclosure for a sacred process. It is an environment in which we can find our actual *center*, that place within us where the forces that influence us come into equilibrium, a place from which our consciousness will go into a natural expansion. Seeing a ceremonial kiva made me look at things that tend to happen in energy healing in a new light. It also renewed my appreciation for the fact that sacred processes require appropriate containment, and when it comes to energy treatments, it is the healer's job to provide that. Here are a few observations coming out of my practice.

When a person goes into a deep state of relaxation, as often happens in treatments, their energy field expands. This expansion of energy creates an oval or egg-shaped form around their body. This seems to be one of the main ways that energy moves: inwards toward a center, and then outward in all directions from that center. We even talk about "centering" in a wide variety of practices like meditation and yoga as a prelude for entering deeper states of consciousness which these practices can open to us. And this is particularly important, of course, in energywork.

During periods of energetic expansion your partner might seem to be "out of her body," that is, she goes into a dreamlike state. Sometimes people daydream during these times, journeying into worlds that are invisible to everyone else. Sometimes they go into states in which they rest deeply in a kind of healing sleep. Or they have insights or experiences relevant to their process of healing and growth.

To sum this idea up, the "energy kiva" is a container for experience, a place of initiation. It is both a place of refuge and the trailhead where you begin your journey. In the energy kiva, healing begins with setting the right conditions for us to make a journey out of our normal bodily consciousness and for the containment of what we draw into our consciousness when we return from that expanded state of awareness. This expansion and journeying, and then returning to a more everyday state of awareness, are events which seem to happen all by themselves once the stage is set in terms of safety and energetic alignment. When this happens, I see myself not so much as a healer but as a kind of guardian for the process at hand. My focus has often much more to do with mindfully and lovingly maintaining this sacred space for my partner while she is doing some important inner work.

"First-Aid Treatment": A Healing Energy Kiva

With this background, let's move now to what I consider to be an extremely handy treatment form to have in your healer's tool kit. The "First-Aid Treatment" has a variety of uses because of the safe, stable healing environment it provides, and because it fulfills, simply and effectively, all the requirements for an energy kiva. It combines some of the most essential elements of healing treatments: geometry, the way the etheric conducts energy, and, very important, your feeling for the person you are treating. Not only is this healing energy kiva wonderful for helping little children to get to sleep, it is effective as a kind of energetic "first-aid" if your partner is in a state of imbalance, emotional upset or even trauma or shock.

This is how you set up the treatment:

Position: Have your partner lie on her *right side*, curled up into a loose fetal position. Many people find this to be a "comfort position." Sit facing your partner so that your left hand is toward her head and your right hand is toward her feet. Stretch out your arms to see if your "wingspan" is wide enough to easily touch your partner's head with your left hand and her feet with your right hand. If you can't make this reach easily, ask your partner to scrunch up a bit into a tighter ball. The hand that is placed on the back of her neck is simply laid over that position. Unless you are extremely short, or working on a huge person, or trying to work on a table that is set too high, this shouldn't be any more difficult than reaching about 18" out from your left pants pocket with your left hand, if you are standing. If you are sitting, make sure the table isn't too high.

Remember that all these contacts are with the energy-active positions associated with these parts of the body. Check the illustrations of this treatment, and if you need to, review the locations of these energy-active positions before you start. They are in the Second Etheric Laboratory: Energy-Active Positions on the Body.

TREATMENT STEPS:

1. **Medulla contact:** Place the palm of your left hand just below the base of the skull on the back of your partner's neck (medulla).

2. **Medulla/joints:** Remembering that it is the natural energetic exchange between your hands that does the work, with your left hand on your partner's medulla, use your right hand to connect, in turn, with the following positions. Take between one and two minutes for each position in order to let the contact build up:

a. **Medulla/your partner's left ankle:** With your right hand, form a "saddle" over her ankle, that is, gently resting your hand, palm down, over the top of her ankle, with your thumb on one side and your fingers on the other. About two minutes.

b. **Medulla/her right ankle:** Repeat the above for the right ankle. About two minutes.

c. **Medulla/her left knee:** Place your right palm on her knee cap. About two minutes.

d. **Medulla/her right knee:** Repeat the above for the right knee. About two minutes.

e. **Medulla/her left hip:** Place your palm so it covers the inside crest of her left hip on the front of her body (see illustration). If you are sitting facing your partner as suggested, this position will feel like you are gently pushing the front of her pelvis away from you. Stay with this contact for about two minutes.

NOTE: Because your partner is lying on her right side, you won't be able to connect her right hip and her right shoulder. Don't worry about them. Just move on to the next available position on her left side.

f. **Medulla/her left shoulder:** Place your right hand on her shoulder so that you are covering her shoulder point with the palm of your hand. About two minutes.

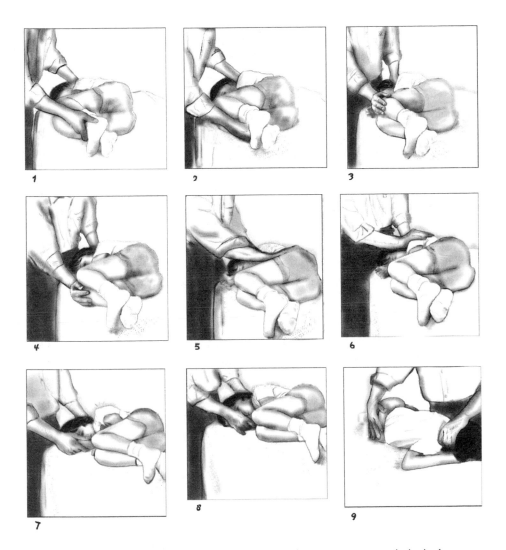

FIRST-AID TREATMENT: When giving this treatment, your left hand remains stationary at the back of your partner's neck while your right hand moves from position to position as shown.

g. **Medulla/her left wrist:** Simply encircle her wrist with your thumb and fingers. Stay with this contact for about two minutes.

h. **Medulla/her right wrist:** Repeat the above for her right wrist.

i. **Medulla/sacrum (tailbone):** What you are doing here is charging the spinal column with energy. This is a good conclusion for the treatment. Unless you have long arms, you might want to move to a position behind your partner and place the palm of your right hand on her medulla, and the palm of your left hand on her sacrum. Let this contact build for about two minutes.

j. **Ending the treatment:** To conclude, ask your partner to rest a bit in whatever position is comfortable to her before getting up. Suggest that when she finally gets up, she should do it slowly, so she won't get dizzy. Stay nearby in case she needs some help "coming back." It is possible that she will want to talk about her experiences, so hopefully you have left a bit of time for that. Equally possible, she might feel the need to go home and rest.

How Does This Treatment Work?

The "First-Aid Treatment" is an easy way to help your partner to come into a state of rest and centering, whether after a hard day at the office, or during a crisis or in the aftermath of other upsetting events. Here are some keys to understanding this treatment: the medulla position at the back of the neck is often very emotionally charged. It is located right behind the Throat Chakra, the energetic switchboard for our avenue of expression. If your partner is emotionally upset, or out of balance when you give her this treatment, you might feel quite a charge at this position; it might even be buzzing or pulsing with energy. When you make an energetic connection between this often overcharged position of the energy field and one of your partner's joints, the result is a dissipation of the energy around the medulla. It flows off in the direction of the joint, which is able to discharge energy much more easily than the medulla. This is easy to understand when you consider that when an area of high concentration is brought into contact with an area of low concentration, there is a tendency for the two areas to equalize. Like water that seeks its own level, the energy held in a highly concentrated area flows off toward less concentrated areas.

Looking at the Geometry of Healing

Let's consider also the kind of geometry we are using in this treatment. Have you noticed that you create a circle with your partner when you make your first contact with your left hand at the back of her neck and your right hand at her feet? I find that there is something about this opening position that communicates a sense of nurture and support to the person I am working on. All you need to do is to make a circle out in front of you with your arms to feel the power of this geometric shape. It is almost impossible to get into some of these positions and not see them as a kind of "energetic gesture." When you create this nurturing circle with another person it is difficult not to open your heart to them and feel them opening their heart to you. Remember the last time you got a sincere hug from a close friend and how it made you feel. This, clearly, is an everyday example of the nurturing quality of a circle.

Another geometric shape, or energetic gesture, that plays a central role in this treatment is the triangle. Think of the medulla position at the back of your partner's neck as the apex and the positions on the left and right sides of her body as the base of a triangle. Many times in energywork, we create triangles which connect positions on either side of the body with positions on the midline. This is because the triangle is the main energetic gesture for balance. When we create a triangle in the energy field, we influence the area inside the triangle in a balancing way.

The "First-Aid Treatment" is good medicine because it makes effective use of the energetic gestures of nurture, centering and balance, all of them important elements for anyone who needs to regroup. In addition to being a good all-around treatment for people when they are upset, wound up and sleepless, I have also found it helpful for people suffering from indigestion, heartburn, menstrual cramps, and headaches. I know of no contraindications for this one. It has a very harmonizing and relaxing effect. I use this treatment, or elements of it, all the time.

Another Side of Creating a Healing Environment

You never know when someone is going to teach you something about healing. After all the talk about meeting the energetic requirements for healing, it is important to bear in mind that these are only guidelines for the healer, things to do which are conducive to healing processes. Sometimes, though, things happen that remind you that healing is not dependent on you setting a perfect stage.

A massage client of mine, Jack, is a stroke patient living full-time in a nursing home. A Korean War vet, bomber pilot. Jack's left arm is completely curled up, his hand a tight spastic ball. Unable to do much at all outwardly, he lies in his hospital bed in a drab room with artificial heating and cooling. Wall-to-wall shelves are filled with videos about warplanes and every modern war. He has videos of every John Wayne film ever made.

During massage the TV is on. The History Channel, mostly war documentaries. Today's selection is the Tet Offensive.

"Jack, do we have to have this on while you're getting a massage?"

"I want it on."

"Only if you insist."

"I insist."

"OK. But if you fall asleep, I'm turning that sumbitch off."

"It's a deal."

We start. I massage both his legs, then move to his chest and his withered left arm. His elbow reminds me of a leftover roast turkey wing, brittle and leathery. Unyielding.

The Vietnam War is booming across the room. Jack and I chat while I work his arm. Our conversation is about war films, obviously an interest of his. I had just seen the film *Saving Private Ryan* and told him about it. I described the realism of the opening combat scene, the "sizz-KLANK!" sound of bullets all around you in the movie theater as you watch the Allied Forces creep forward on Omaha Beach under massive gunfire.

Suddenly Jack interrupts me. "Yeah, and they tell you in infantry training that if your buddy next to you is hit, you just keep on going . . ."

Then he lets out a gasp and a sob, ". . . and I just couldn't do that!"

And at that moment, as he sobs, his left arm lets go, softens and straightens out. In amazement we stare at one another, at his arm, and back at each other.

By and by, Jack's left arm ratchets itself back into the position it had been in for years. As we complete the massage, however, Jack is in a kind of peace and relaxation I had not seen before with him. I leave with a new appreciation for what the human spirit will do to heal itself.

I had no way of knowing exactly what experience had come up inside him at that moment his arm loosened. I did understand, though, that Jack had unconsciously surrounded himself with what he needed to be on *his* path of healing. Jack's war memorabilia-filled room certainly didn't match *my* idea of an energy kiva or an ideal "healing environment," but who am I to determine that for anyone else? It was a powerful reminder that when a person is ready to take a step in their healing process, it will happen.

Sometimes, the energy kiva that allows the person to feel safe is very different from what we might deliberately design for them. Most of the time, however, it is true that offering an energy kiva that is nurturing and relaxing will be what works most consistently. Even as you hold this model in your mind, leave room for the possibility that maybe your treatment partner needs a blaring TV set playing in the background, or some other distraction which you find annoying. Some people's defenses dissolve slowly, indeed, and they must drop those defenses before they are able to enter the gentler, more vulnerable place of healing that you offer. Jack felt safe with the images and sounds of war thundering in the background. Do what you can to create the nurturing environment but leave space for folks like Jack as well.

The "First-Aid Treatment"
AT A GLANCE

POSITION: Have your partner lie on her *right side*, curled up into a loose fetal position. Many people find this to be a "comfort position."

Treatment Steps:
1. Medulla contact
2. Medulla/joints
    a. Medulla/your partner's left ankle
    b. Medulla/her right ankle
    c. Medulla/her left knee
    d. Medulla/her right knee
    e. Medulla/her left hip
    f. Medulla/her left shoulder
    g. Medulla/her left wrist
    h. Medulla/her right wrist
    i. Medulla/sacrum (tailbone)
    j. End the treatment

FOURTH ETHERIC LABORATORY
HEALING THE ETHERIC

I. THE NATURE OF THE ETHERIC

ONE OF THE important jobs of the etheric is the distribution of energy around and through the physical. The chakra system, energy-active points and streams are situated in the etheric and play an active role in this distribution network. When we consciously connect with a chakra—that is to say, when we make a feeling contact with the energy movement of the chakra—it has an immediate effect on the entire etheric. The chakras are always active and charged with energy (unless we are dead), but the addition of our conscious awareness to the chakra's activity steps up the pace at which the chakra mediates energy and consciousness. Think of a flower opening its petals to drink in the energy from the sun. Of course, that sunlight-energy has to go through a number of changes in the process of photosynthesis before it is of use to the living cells of the flower. Likewise, one of the main roles played by our chakras is the transformation of life-force, or *prana,* into energy that can be absorbed and used in our life processes.

In simple form this is the pathway of the life-force from the chakras into our bodies: When a chakra is energized, it feeds that energy via the etheric webwork called the "nadis" into the nervous system. These nadis are the subtle-body counterpart of the nervous system and "step down" the frequency of the life-force to that which our physical nerves

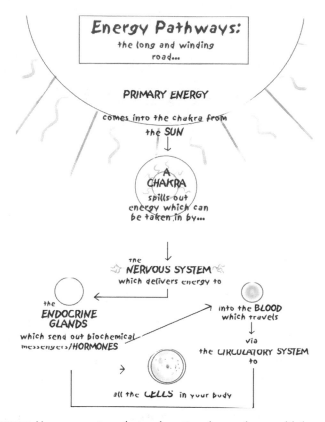

Energy Pathways:
the long and winding
road...

PRIMARY ENERGY

comes into the chakra from
the SUN

A
CHAKRA
spills out
energy which can
be taken in by...

The
NERVOUS SYSTEM
which delivers energy to

the
ENDOCRINE
GLANDS
which send out biochemical
messengers/HORMONES

into the BLOOD
which travels

via
the CIRCULATORY SYSTEM
to

all the CELLS in your body

ENERGY PATHWAYS: Here, you can trace the transformation of energy from raw life force into forms of energy that can be used by our physical bodies.

can accommodate. Each of the primary chakras is linked, through the nadis and nerves, to an endocrine gland. The energization of a chakra sends energy into its respective endocrine gland whose secretion of hormones into the bloodstream influences the body at the cellular level. Although this goes on all the time unconsciously, we enhance this process when we work with the chakras and the energy field in a purposeful, healing way.

The body is full of stories. Each new event in the tribe's history is recorded with a metal wedge or nail which is driven into the body of this figure from the Republic of Congo. The tribe's storyteller can point to each "story nail" and tell the history of the tribe.

The Holographic Property of the Etheric

Most of us tend to view the physical body as a collection of parts and separate systems—circulatory, respiratory, reproductive, etc. Given our cultural penchant for breaking everything down into its components, it is difficult to think of a human as a whole. Furthermore, we divide ourselves up into body, mind, emotion and spirit, and each of these divisions has its own set of subdivisions. I would certainly agree that it seems to make things easier to understand if we pretend that it is possible to break the body down into various components and study each one as if it were separate and autonomous. But the etheric doesn't let us get away with that kind of thinking. It demands that we expand our awareness and stretch our minds to think holographically.

A hologram is a three-dimensional "photograph" which contains the image of the whole in each of its parts. The word "hologram" is derived from the Greek *holos*, meaning "whole," and *gramma*, meaning something written or recorded. In the three-dimensional photographic process called "holography," you can actually take a holographic plate with, let's say, the image of an armadillo on it, break it into numerous pieces, and still project the image of the *whole armadillo* from each piece. At least theoretically, you can then take one of the pieces, grind it up in a pencil-sharpener, and project the image of the entire armadillo from any one of its infinite particles. In holographic photography, the projected image of the armadillo gets less and less crisp as the pieces get smaller, but still, the entire image is contained in every point in the medium.

In the consciousness research of Karl Pribram, back in the 1960s, he theorized that each particle of gray matter in our brains worked holographically as well. To create an image of an armadillo in our mind's eye was to set into motion holographic events throughout our nervous systems, activating energy throughout our entire beings.

William Blake said he saw the whole world in a grain of sand, a holographic statement if there ever was one. What I love most about healing work are the transparent moments of connection with the cosmos through connection with people. Humans are my grain of sand. There are moments when the whole universe seems to be revealed wherever I happen to turn my attention. In this regard, energywork has an unmistakable touch of the holographic about it, with the energyworker a witness to the whole show. Though we might be linking with but a single energy-active position in a personal exercise or a treatment we give, an image of a person's entire energy system can open to us.

In a certain limited way, we can get away, temporarily, with a fragmented (non-holographic) approach to our lives. After all, we do take the various "parts" of ourselves to specialists: we take our teeth to the dentist, our muscles and skin to our massage therapist, our heads to Dr. Freud and our souls to Father Duffy. But, as necessary as it might be, this "farming out" of parts of ourselves cultivates our sense of being fragmented. Behind the scenes, though, we have much more in common with this holographic armadillo. No matter how much we grind ourselves up into little pieces, something of our wholeness can be found in each of our parts. Energywork is a direct link to the holographic level of our organization, and the etheric is its first easily available level.

Inner and Outer Influences That Affect the Etheric

The etheric is essentially a *fluid, vibrating light structure.* Rudolph Steiner, the philosopher scientist who founded the Anthroposophic movement, referred to "etheric formative forces" and identified four levels of the etheric body. As a light structure, it has an affinity for all that behaves like light and energy. Therefore, it contracts and expands, and reacts to sound and color, to rhythm and pulsation. It also has an affinity for the formative powers of light, which express in the geometric patterns which light produces. There are other ways of describing the etheric, but this will get us started.

To know something about what influences the etheric, for better or for worse, is to gather the keys for unlocking the secrets for working with energy in a healing mode. If we were to do a personal energy exercise, for example the "Etheric Body-Stocking in Basic Etheric Navigation Exercise #3", every day for two weeks, we would find that there are definite differences in the etheric from day to day. Some days, the exercise might be easy and feel great. Other days we might

What has a Damaging Effect on the Etheric?

- Stress
- Loud, Sudden Sound
- Repressed Emotion/
  Lack of Expression
- Shock, Trauma

All of these can disrupt the natural rhythm and flow of the etheric and create areas of blockage. Shock and trauma can lead to encapsulations or "energy cysts."

What has a Positive Effect on the Etheric?

- Light
- Color
- Water
- Sound
- Rhythm

- Touch
- Love and Compassion
- Contact with Nature
- Prayer
- Breath
- Harmonious Geometry

These Elements Encourage the Etheric Body to Act According to its Nature

Rhythm and Sound	encourage	Pulsation (Expansion and Contraction)
Color and Light	encourage	Light Vibration
Geometry and Music	encourage	Order and Harmony
Nature and Water	encourage	Cyclic Flow
Ritual, Observance of Moon and Celestial Cycles, Breath	encourage	Interaction with Cosmos

wonder if we even have an etheric, or we might feel like we are slog-
ging along waist-deep through muddy fields.

Experience of the etheric varies as our physical, emotional and
mental states change. The health and resilience of our etheric body
will also affect how we experience it. Moon cycles and seasons of the
year, the amount of sunlight and water we are exposed to, the food we
eat and the other substances we introduce into our system will all con-
tribute to the state of the etheric.

The Effects of Medications and Drugs on the Etheric Body

There is a seemingly infinite number of agents both inside and outside our bodies which can have an effect on the etheric. Some of these
are very subtle, such as the color in the decor of a store, or the fact that
we are aware of a buzzing sound in the next room which is causing us
to feel irritated. Others are far from subtle, such as the disruption of
the etheric following a car accident in which we have had serious
physical injuries. While we would certainly expect the latter to have
a powerful impact it is easy to overlook other powerful influences, if
only because they are such a "normal" part of contemporary life. An
example of this is the use of drugs—prescription and otherwise.
Some, such as aspirin, are quite benign for most people but affect others quite profoundly. In any case, whenever we start working at an
etheric level we need to be aware of both subtle and gross influences
of drugs.

It is not my intention here to give the impression that all medica-
tions or other drugs can cause irreparable harm. Many healers who
work in the energy field do, however, wring their hands when they
learn that a partner is taking a lot of medication, whether doctor-pre-
scribed or self-prescribed. Not that it is impossible for them to be
helpful as healers if a partner is heavily medicated, but they know, for
example, that drugs and substances we put into our bodies, such as
powerful pharmaceuticals, alcohol, tobacco, amphetamines
("uppers"), tranquilizers ("downers"), anti-depressants and psychedelics do complicate the energyworker's job and there is little doubt
that the habitual use of certain chemical substances sets real limitations on a person's ability to benefit consciously from an energyworker's treatments.

Drugs that act on the nervous system, change normal rhythms such as heartbeat or hormonal secretions, or which alter consciousness, can make personal energy exercises and meditation difficult. These drugs tend to either desensitize or oversensitize a person's subtle sensory system. The reason for this is simple. Each substance we take into our bodies has its own energetic aspect which alters the rhythms of the energy field. In general, man-made chemicals, as well as some natural ones, can tamper with the movement of the energy field by slowing it down; the energetic aspect of the chemicals moves more slowly than the energy field, which is a light structure. Contrasting areas of density, and patches of movement slower than that of surrounding areas then show in the energy field.

Psychedelics, such as LSD, peyote, psilocybin, and mescaline influence the etheric in some very specific ways. They must be understood in energy healing because so many people growing up in our culture, particularly during the 1960s through the 1980s, have taken these drugs at one time or another. Psychedelics were popular with tens of thousands of people who experimented with altered states of consciousness.

Cultural anthropologists tell us that these drugs were used in the context of sacred ritual, within some of the world's oldest religions— i.e. the earliest shamanic traditions—and, much later, even with contemplative Christian and Kabbalistic sects. But within those traditions the use of drugs was integrated with sophisticated and rigorous religious and ethical teachings.

Part of the problem with using these substances "recreationally," is that people can experience a radical change of consciousness but have no way of integrating their experiences into their lives. Without the spiritual background to give a positive context to the insights and shifts of consciousness triggered by these substances, people often ended up more bewildered about life than ever, and in some cases were deeply wounded.

Much depends on the context. There are significant differences between, say, a Native American who takes part in a peyote ceremony in the Native American Church[1], after having been prepared for

[1] The Native American Church is the official church organization that has federal protection for the legal use of peyote.

the experience and watched over by tribal elders in the context of age-old spiritual traditions, and a person who takes psychedelics in an excessive and injudicious way for mind-blowing entertainment. The ceremonial use of the psychedelic substance in the first instance is neither excessive nor random, and is contained in a ceremonial environment, often within a ceremonial community, and is accompanied by prayers for guidance and wisdom.

A person's energy field can carry the residue of drug use long after they have stopped using it. While many pharmaceutical drugs restrict the natural movement and expansion of the etheric by slowing it down and blocking its activity, psychedelics can have the effect of adding more energy to the etheric than it can process, speeding up and exaggerating some of its processes. Remember that the etheric acts as a bridge between the physical body and other energy dimensions which surround it. It has a subtle "skin," or semipermeable membrane around it. The layers of energetic activity in and around the body—and bear in mind that these layers are the storehouse of the various levels of the subconscious—are intended to *interact and blend*, but not to wash in and out of one another indiscriminately, as can happen with some so-called "consciousness expanding" drugs. Therefore, while the etheric body is able to expand, sudden additions of large amounts of energy to it can cause a premature, imbalanced expansion, causing it to stretch out of shape, develop energetic cysts, lesions, tears and cracks, even lacunae or holes. I will have more to say about etheric wounding as we look at other factors along the way.

Bomb-Sitting and Energetic Constipation

The etheric reacts to how we express ourselves, or hold back on expressing. We have all kinds of reasons, it seems, for regulating the expression of our feelings—from editing what we really feel so as to not hurt others to trying to remain outwardly consistent with images and expectations we have created in the past, from putting on our smiley face or our poker face and not expressing what is inside us, to outright denial that anything is going on under the surface at all. From an energetic standpoint, these blocks to self-expression manifest in two different ways: 1) repression, or holding back what would otherwise be expressed, and 2) being dishonest about what we do express; expressing outwardly something that is radically *different* from what is going on inside us. In both cases, our expression ends up being incongruent with our inner reality.

Let's bear in mind that all the contents of our inner lives, whether thoughts or feelings, are *primarily energy*. Although they may change states, they remain energy, just as water may appear as ice one moment and steam the next, and still remain water. That means that even if we repress something to the point of totally forgetting it, it still exists in the background as an energetic pattern. It continues to play a role in our life experience even though it does so at an unconscious level. Energetic patterns attract and organize energy, which means that even our best-hidden secrets, and things we may have totally forgotten, continue to shape how we experience our lives.

Energy is neither created nor destroyed.

FIRST LAW OF THERMODYNAMICS

There is a huge difference between emotion that is allowed to express and emotion that is kept from expressing. We are using the word "emotion" in its broadest sense, as that which wants to "move out" from us (e-motion = motion outward). When it comes to healing, chronic problems do not arise so much from emotions *per se* as from the *fear-based repression of emotions,* which causes what would naturally be ex-pressed (pushed outward) to be sup-pressed (pushed downward) into the energetic system.

Etheric Splitting

The etheric bears the energetic consequences, both large and small, of what we are doing, expressing or not expressing, in short, of who we are at any one point in time. An absolute "match" between our inner and outer experience of life is probably impossible. Even the most honest person is not completely transparent at all times. Perhaps it is not even wise to try to have total congruence between inner and outer. There are times, after all, when telling the truth can get us in trouble.

We do whatever is necessary to protect our spirit, especially during vulnerable times when we are in a healing process or entering a new phase of our life, such as puberty or menopause. Like a mother bird camouflaging her nest or luring predators away from her nesting babies, we naturally develop strategies for protecting tender newborn parts of ourselves—while presenting to the world an outer façade of something else—so they can grow in peace. Adolescence is a universal example of a period of clash between inner and outer worlds. The adolescent boy hides *Playboy* pictures in his Bible; as his fascination with his budding manly feelings gives way to the study of religion, he might go through a period of doing just the opposite: the Bible and the *Playboy* might switch places. This kind of thing seems to be part of growing—necessary, but not without its awkwardness and confusion. Interestingly, it is often the skin, that interfacing boundary between the inside and outside of a person (and generally a good indicator of the condition of the etheric), that takes quite a hit during that pubescent time of learning how to relate to other people and the outside world.

While a certain amount of duplicity may be a necessary pretext for survival or growth, we nevertheless create conflict and energetic clash when we talk out of both sides of our mouths on subjects that are important to us, or when we do things which violate our deepest beliefs. The real issue here is congruency; we suffer if we go too long without it.

It could be said that we all live a "double life" to some extent, but what actually happens energetically when a serious discrepancy between inner and outer is prolonged? Most of us have had the experience of telling a little white lie that breeds deception and slowly grows into a fiction that requires a good deal of energy to maintain. For example, maybe we continue year after year in a profession or a relationship or a lifestyle which down deep we know is not compatible with who we really are. At mid-life, we look around us and see a world full of missed callings, unexplored passions and spiritual gifts: the artist or healer who finds herself stuck in a job that saps her energy but doesn't satisfy her deepest inner calling; the gay person who pretends to be straight, or the straight person who pretends to be gay; the person in the midst of illness or upheaval who acts as if everything were just peachy; the corporate executive who can't give up the job he hates because he and his family like the money he earns. We all know about these incongruities.

Ray was HIV+ and came to me regularly for energywork. In our sessions, I was curious to find layers of intense energy activity well away from Ray's body, and another focus of intense energy activity inside his body, which I contacted just under the skin surface. Between these two areas of activity was a kind of gap or "empty zone." The inner and outer layers of the etheric appeared to have separated.

Ray told me that he had not ever let his parents know he was on welfare or that he was gay, let alone that he was HIV+ or that he was caring for his lover who was dying of AIDS. For years he had maintained an elaborate fiction for his parents, presenting himself as a straight man with a regular job. Ray was a walking contradiction, presenting a rough exterior, with knocked-out teeth, scarred complexion and self-administered tattoos with misspelled words. Yet he revealed himself to me as a person with a refined sense of spirituality and beauty, who wrote poetry, painted and lovingly cared for his partner.

Because the etheric forms the threshold between our inner and outer consciousness, this layer also reflects the way our inner and outer worlds interact. Ray's example was the most extreme case of "etheric splitting" that I have encountered in a person who was also quite conscious of his situation. Ray was well aware of the huge paradoxes and contradictions in his life but felt unable to do anything about them. Not surprisingly, the tension he experienced was enormous. Ray showed up regularly over a six-month period for energy treatments and worked diligently with energy exercises I showed him. In the work we did together, which focused on healing the etheric, a couple of things began to happen. First, he acknowledged the absurdity of his enormous contradictions and what it was costing him in terms of his health and peace of mind. He also began to talk to me about his beliefs and share spiritual experiences he had. It seemed that at the same time he was facing his desperation about the bind he was in, he was also calling on inner resources of comfort, guidance and light. We talked about how he might live in greater alignment with his beliefs and eventually developed a course of action to do just that. At one point, I noticed a change in the quality of his etheric. Though the "gap" was still quite palpable, it had began to shrink. The space between his body and the energy activity around him was not as empty as it had been, and this corresponded to his making some important decisions, including his sharing more about his life with his parents.

Healing the Etheric

Our ability to focus our attention is a powerful skill in energywork. *Attention* plays a dual role of projecting energy and awareness to an area of our body where we are experiencing problems or to other people who have come to us for healing. Though we draw to ourselves all kinds of energetic influences semiconsciously or totally unconsciously, we can also take the process of self-healing in hand by deliberately exposing the etheric to elements which promote its health. What we pay attention to affects our etheric and, as the exercises in this book demonstrate, when we turn our attention to the etheric itself, healing processes can be set in motion.

The etheric is in constant flux and change. One way of understanding the meaning of the "physical/etheric interface" is to consider that this is the field, or semipermeable membrane, where our external or environmental influences meet with our internal life. We are referring to this when we say a person is "thin-skinned" if she is extremely sensitive and reactive to what goes on around her. The opposite is true if she is "thick-skinned," unresponsive to her environment.

Alongside the role played by the nervous system in the physical body, the etheric is the vehicle for our kinesiological sense of body-feeling, and therefore for the senses. Just as water conducts electricity, *the etheric conducts energy and consciousness,* and this includes impressions we take in from non-physical sources. This capability of the etheric makes "ESP" possible, except that is not so much "extra"-sensory perception we are talking about, but rather *extended* sensory perception.

The etheric is definitely *elastic.* To imagine the etheric as a uniform sheath of energy a neat and constant inch or so away from the skin surface is erroneous. In some places it is hugged in tight to the skin where there is little awareness, or even drawn into the body, in the case of injury. Elsewhere, there is an expansion well out from the body, something which takes place between lovers, in meditative states and also in the energy fields of healers when they are at work.

Let's look at some everyday examples of this. Two people meet, come into conversation and hit upon topics they are both passionate about. Soon they are "enmeshed," deep in intense conversation. Energetically, that period of enmeshment is characterized by an expansion of their energy fields. For a while, their fields merge and they seem to create their own private bubble of communication. Another obvious example is two people who fall in love. Another would be a teacher who comes into an intense rapport with her students on a subject she cares intensely about. She may be standing in front of her class, but she seems to reach out and touch everyone in the room and each student feels she is speaking directly to him or her. In each of these examples, the energy field, and especially that aspect we call the etheric, shows a remarkable ability to expand.

The opposite type of movement, namely *contraction,* is also in evidence in the etheric. Think of the times when a person "shrinks" from something, recoils in disgust or feels repelled, withdraws, disengages, or simply loses interest in something. Here, we see examples of feelings that are accompanied by etheric contraction. Similarly, when a person is frightened or physically or emotionally injured the etheric tends to be hugged in close to the body. Whether we open ourselves up, or close ourselves off, we seem to do it in the etheric first, even before our words and actions make it obvious.

The etheric has layers which need to communicate with one another. These can become "unglued;" that is to say, the inner and outer layers separate, resulting in a kind of "etheric split." A typical situation in which this occurs is when there is a gross discrepancy between a person's inner and outer life, like what I described earlier with my client Ray. The usual point of contact between the inner and outer layers of the etheric is the skin surface, which provides us with an excellent means of affecting the physical/etheric interface.

While giving an energy treatment, you may sense that the main activity is inside the person's body. Or you may sense that it is well off the skin surface. If the energy activity is predominately inside the body, as may be the case with a person who is in fear or hurt, closed off or in a strongly repressed state, it is likely that the strength of activity is concentrated in the etheric layers that penetrate the body.

Knowing that energy responds to intention, what I do as I touch this area is to "invite" that activity out to the skin surface so it can reconnect with the external layers of the etheric. It is a little like silently beckoning to a friend, who is standing across the room, to come join you where you are sitting. Here, I do a bit of creative visualization to go along with my silent invitation; I see my fingers magnetically drawing those inner energy layers out to the surface, or I see my fingers covered with Velcro reaching into the body and attaching to these layers so I can very gently pull them out.

If you sense energetic activity predominantly outside the body, beyond the skin surface, this means that the etheric—and the person's consciousness—can probably go quite easily into an expanded state. A lack of connection here is most likely a sign of an impaired ability to ground the energies that are available in those expanded states in the body. A typical difficulty for persons in such a condition is that their insights do not easily translate into actions; the connection to everyday life is weak. This might be the situation with persons who live in their heads or in their ideals and fantasies. Here, again, the idea is to help with the reconnection of these inner and outer layers of the etheric at the skin surface. The "invitation" that I communicate through my hands is for the external layer of the etheric to come back to the skin surface. In the first case, we are expanding the etheric beyond the physical; in the second, we are grounding the etheric in the body.

Restrictive Belief Structures

Because energy follows your mind, your intentions and beliefs, attitudes and worldviews have a profound affect on the etheric. To understand how this works, we have to make the distinction between mutable, superficial attitudes or opinions, and the deep belief structures that form the bedrock of our reality. Our beliefs tend to mediate our experience; that is, we behave differently toward something we believe is real than we do toward something we do not believe is real. One of the joys of watching a magician or sleight-of-hand artist is that we can sense the contours of our beliefs about everyday realities. A woman appears to be sawed in half before our eyes, and though we know that it didn't really happen, we are still somehow slightly relieved when the magician finishes the trick by showing us that she is, after all, still intact.

Whether our beliefs are flirted with by a David Copperfield magic show or Hollywood special effects, or blown apart by experiences that completely change how we see the world, they are a strong part of our makeup. The more unconscious and unquestioned they are, the more influence they can have.

Any belief structure that is basically a rigid, absolute hold on "the way things are" will inhibit etheric expansion and flexibility. Some mental and emotional habits can take on this kind of rigidity, often showing up as a lack of imagination, or as "isms" such as fanaticism, pessimism, determinism, and fatalism. Add to these our seemingly endless list of obsessions, fixations, judgments, self-criticisms, guilts and self-reproaches and we have quite a collection of restrictive belief structures. All of these have at least one thing in common: they show up in the energy field as energy patterns and limit the etheric's natural tendency to expand and form a bridge between higher, progressive states of consciousness and everyday life. The energy healer is in a position to help restore the etheric to healthy function. In doing so, she will energetically encounter the things which hinder its expansion.

Trauma, Shock, and Injury

We are all born with the ability to protect ourselves when we are overwhelmed. Traumatized body parts or emotions become desensitized or numb; a whole person becomes insensitive, closed off, or, in extreme cases, comatose. The process of going into shock, with all the attendant processes of dissociation, can be necessary for survival. Think of all the things that happen which are well nigh impossible to go through and stay completely conscious and present. Many events, from sudden impact and pain, loud sound, threat of danger, to all the varieties of abuse, trigger the "fight or flight" arousal of the sympathetic nervous system, and very often, the flight is away from the body and its sensations. Whether we experience this forced exit from consciousness for an hour or an instant, we still sustain a wound and the energetic component of that wound is held in the etheric. In a process analogous to that of a physical wound, "energy cysts," or encapsulations can form where damaged areas are sheathed in a protective cocoon until healing can take place.

"Energy cyst" is a very useful term which my wife Ursula began using a few years back. It describes what we felt to be cyst-like encapsulations on the energetic level. We then found that the term is also a piece of the jargon used by John Upledger in his craniosacral teaching. Upledger said he first heard it from Elmer Green, the founder of the Biofeedback Department at the Menninger Foundation.

Energy cysts are localized, encapsulated zones of "chaotic" energy. Typically, an energy cyst forms in the human energy field when there is trauma and injury. This can come about in a variety of ways, through: impact and actual damage to the tissue; emotional trauma; overuse; disease; surgical procedures; and sudden emotional shock. We all experience these things in our lives. The energy cyst follows the same basic patterns as any wound. It represents a zone where too much energy has entered the system. The system can't dissipate the energy in its normal way, so it encapsulates it in order to keep it from spreading out and compromising the whole system.

Sometimes, in the process of working with another person, you feel drawn to a specific area of the body. You notice a variation in the vibration. In all likelihood it is a disturbance pattern, or energy cyst, that is showing up on your "radar." Some areas are more dense than their surroundings; they vibrate more slowly, especially in places where there is a physical or emotional wound of some kind. The energy metabolism of the area is slower and the energy patterns are less ordered, more "confused." Typically, they are in areas of the body and energy field which, when addressed in treatments, bring forward experiences of unresolved events from the past. Bear in mind that this energy, which moves around and

> *"In order for a person to heal, the body/mind needs to be spoken to in its own language, the language of light, color, sound, archetype and feeling, so that it can learn to vibrate again in harmony with all of creation."*
>
> URSULA GILKESON

within the body, is where the subconscious record of your experiences is stored.

It is not unusual that interventions as simple as placing your hands on such an area of the body, or sandwiching the area between your hands and allowing the energetic exchange between your hands to take place, can help to initiate release of an energy cyst. Release might happen rapidly or over a period of time. If the original trauma has been severe and emotional, short repeated treatments can be very helpful, allowing the release to come a little at a time, letting the person integrate the changes gradually. The disorganized pocket of energy is allowed to come, in its own time and in its own way, back into the normal flow of energy in and around the body.

It is important to recognize that a release can also be quite monumental, taking a variety of forms. In people with strong, unresolved trauma or long-repressed feelings, energy healing can uncover long-repressed memories. If you are new to energy work and unfamiliar with deep release, take whatever time you need to become familiar with energy exercises and treatments before going at it with other people. To responsibly work on others, it is imperative that you be comfortable with emotional release, and that begins with your own. There are now numerous programs for counselors and bodyworkers that offer instruction in the release of emotion. In the chapter on "Exercises with a Release Phase," I will go into this very important subject some more.

The activation of the etheric will tend to cause us to encounter anything that is unresolved in energetic terms. That could be an unhealed wound, a decision you didn't carry out, a conflict, a grudge, birth trauma, any process that for whatever reason has not come full circle. It is typical to hear a person who is working on their inner development say, "I thought I had already gotten that behind me." By which they mean they have probably already figured something out on a rational level, perhaps done some emotional processing and made their peace with an issue. Then, because it is still an energy pattern in the background, they run smack into it in their energy field in the course of bodywork or energywork. It is inevitable. The good news is that when an energetic pattern finally clears—usually after numerous releases of what has accumulated around that pattern—then a truly new pattern can enter in.

Breathing Together: My Conspiracy with a Tibetan Lama

It's time now for a little story about how I learned something that I now use regularly in energywork. I call it my "conspiracy" because of the interesting Latin derivation of that word. To "conspire" comes from the Latin word *conspirare*, which is made up of *com-*, together, + *spirare*, to breathe.

In 1980 I visited a friend in Sweden who had been selected by the Tibetan Buddhist Temple in Stockholm to be the official doctor for a three-year, three-month, three-week, three-day retreat which would be starting soon. Although Meri herself was not a retreatant, she had to be initiated into the retreat so that she could be among those few from the outside world allowed to enter the hermitage while it was closed.

I was invited to visit the temple with her. While I meditated in the puja room with its wild array of benevolent and scary faces on the wall, a temple resident tapped me on the shoulder and asked if I would like to meet Lama Nawang. I said I definitely would.

The little Lama led me up a ladder to an attic loft which was his quarters. We had no common language. I spoke no Tibetan and he spoke no more than a few words in any Western language that I knew. So there we sat, I on a creaky chair, he in a lotus position on his army cot, between us a tiny Salvation Army coffee table with a pot of tea and a couple of cookies. We stared at each other until he broke the silence.

"Drink Tibetan tea!"

I did. It had butter in it and smelled of goat. Later I was told it was yak butter. When I stopped, he repeated, louder, "DRINK TIBETAN TEA!" He repeated this a number of times. Each time he said it, I jumped, startled by the penetration of his voice.

"DRINK TIBETAN TEA!!" The way he said it seemed to have nothing to do with drinking tea.

Then we stopped drinking Tibetan tea and stared at each other. I had no idea what was coming. Lama Nawang's eyes became intense. He took a sudden deep breath through his nose and held it. Reflexively, so did I. He let it out though his mouth and I followed him. Another breath, deep and intense, and then another. Some were loud, some released with a burst of air. Each time I copied him.

This continued. At some point, I stopped copying. It seemed he was still initiating the breath each time, but there was no more lag between his breathing and mine. This simultaneous, identical breathing was suddenly an intense communication between us. At first, Lama Nawang was "breathing" me, so to speak, but as this progressed, it was as if we were both being "breathed."

I now use this idea of "breathing" another person in bodywork. Often in bodywork, when consciously re-connecting with injury or trauma in the body, a person will stop breathing. Quite literally, a part of their body has become "frightened." The response, almost universally, is the same as when any of us are startled: we—in this case, a part of our body—hold our breath. The release of such a pattern includes a release of the patterned response of stopping breathing. What I do is encourage the person I am treating to keep breathing. Often they are not even conscious that they had stopped. I underline the new pattern by breathing slightly audibly with them, following Lama Nawang's lesson to me in Stockholm. Just as women who live close together will tend to fall into the same menstrual cycle, the effect of my "modeling" is that my partner will spontaneously match my rhythm and shift into another breathing pattern.

Re-Inhabiting the Body

Ideally, a healing process promotes a re-inhabitation of the body, that is, the gradual re-entry into areas of injury that a person may have abandoned. What happens to consciousness in people who are in car accidents, children who are mistreated, people who are overwhelmed physically, emotionally or sexually, persons confronted with war and personally devastating turns of events? In her essay *The Wound, the Wall, and the Mask*, homeopath Ananda Zaren describes the process as follows:

> A psychic *wound* is a state of severe fright that ensues when an individual is confronted with a *traumatic experience that is sudden, unexpected, and potentially life-threatening.* [Italics mine.] It is an experience over which the individual has no control and to which he is unable to respond effectively to deflect the event. Examples of this type of trauma include having one's

house destroyed by a fire or natural disaster, being permanently injured as the result of an automobile accident, or being physically or sexually abused by a parent. Individuals can also be *wounded* by witnessing violence. During the event, emergency physiological response systems are activated: heart, lungs, and muscles work at top efficiency. Attention, concentration, and memory become acute, to enable the individual to focus on coping with the threat and preserving life. *In this process, there is a detachment from ordinary reality; microseconds of experience take on altered associations, and a meaningful sense of life becomes disrupted.* [Italics mine.] These are normal reactions to stressful events. Within a few weeks, the fear and confusion is lessened, and the experience can be digested and understood. If the experience cannot be processed in a calm and supportive environment, or if the experience is repeated, the *wound* will not be resolved and the organism will therefore begin to make adaptive changes by creating a *wall* around the *wound*.

The Geometry, Sound, and Color of Energy Healing

Among the many influences on the etheric are some very subtle ones we wouldn't necessarily suspect. Among these are geometry, sound, and color. These influences also give us keys to working with the etheric.

The etheric responds to *shape and geometry*. Consider the effect which shapes in our architecture have on us. After living for our entire lives in boxy houses and rooms full of right angles, no wonder we feel different—and go different places in our consciousness—under the arching canopy of a cathedral or mosque, or under the azure dome of the sky itself. For this reason, it is interesting to go into houses intentionally built without right angles, such as those designed according to anthroposophic principles. They have a completely different "feel" to them.

Symbols which make use of geometric form—especially the square, circle, triangle and semi-circle—have a powerful effect when placed by visualization at specific locations in the energy field. These are the rudimentary shapes of light geometry. Each plays a structural role in the makeup of the etheric and illustrates ways that energy moves between dimensions. They guide energy movement and structure the dynamic forms that energy congeals into as it becomes solid.

Geometric symbols turn out, therefore, to be specific tools for healing the etheric, and working with the energy field in general. For
example, a triangle visualized in specific positions in the energy field
tends to bring into equilibrium what is inside them. An upward-
pointing (toward the head) triangle tends to activate energetic
processes inside it; a downward-pointing triangle (toward the feet)
tends to calm those same processes, bringing about a grounding effect
that allows for the drawing in of elements from higher dimensions of
consciousness. The interpenetration of a downward and an upward-
pointing triangle, the Star of David, creates a powerful effect when
placed specifically in the energy field, as it configures a balanced
interdimensional blending.

A circle with a dot in the middle has a different effect on consciousness; it illustrates another aspect of energy movement. For
example, a circle or sphere illustrates—that is to say, it shows a map
or picture—of energy movement in its expansion out from a center,
then back to that center. It is an energy environment in which a person can center, become calm, open, build up enough sense of safety to
make a shift into a more expansive mode of awareness. The process of
centering is one that the circle, or sphere, accommodates especially
well.

We find our own center when we link our awareness with the energy and consciousness that is moving away from our center and then
back to it. Mindful breathing—a circular activity because it repeats
itself in a cycle—is an age-old example of this kind of practice.

Another category of etheric influence is *sound and rhythm*. It is
probably intuitively obvious to even the most casual observer that if
you spend the day chanting the AUM with your meditation group,
then go out that evening to a rock concert, your energy system will
need some time to go through a radical shift from one set of vibrations
to the other. It's because the etheric is highly reactive to sound. Music,
mantra, sound and word are well known for their effects on the energy field. We frequently used gongs, singing bowls and Tibetan bells
in workshops in Germany. Certain participants were propelled
instantly into vivid memories of their childhood in World War II.
The impact of air raids, the wail of sirens, and the thumping of explo-
sions in the distance were still in their energy fields.

Color and light make up another category of etheric influences. The color schemes in public places can tell you a lot about the activities and intentions of the place. The predominant reds and oranges, activating colors, of a chain discount store would seem out of place in a funeral parlor, wouldn't they? There is a lot of lore about the "meaning" of colors, but we are more interested in looking at colors in terms of what happens when a color is specifically placed in the energy field, that is, a color vibration is introduced into a chakra or some other energy-active position. Each color influences the energy field in a different way; each color's wavelength and vibrational pattern has properties which might either activate, calm, bring inner activity "forward" toward consciousness and expression, or shift consciousness to another dimension. Some of the exercises offered in this book use color in this way. See in particular the "Ms. Chakra" exercises.

Colors are extremely useful in subtle energy practice because they do an "end-run" around the ego; that is, they can't really be manipulated. Once introduced into the energy field, they will do their own thing, but because they are light, they will produce healing effects, either by drawing into the foreground areas of consciousness that were "hiding," or by providing a vehicle for the movement of your consciousness.

Etheric Circulation: Waiting for the Potatoes

Many people have the idea that in order to work effectively with the energy field, they must objectively see it and the movement of energy, but this isn't necessarily true. Considering all the ways that impressions come to us—through all of our senses, by observing our partner's mood and the tension in the various areas their body, and even through our psychic or clairvoyant insights—we shouldn't limit ourselves to a cookbook approach. For example, don't jump to the conclusion that because you saw red in a person's energy field that they are feeling anger. There can, after all, be many reasons for red to appear. By far the larger issue is *assembling those impressions into something useful.* Instead of jumping to conclusions about what your impressions might mean, wait for them to speak for themselves. They will if you are patient and allow all the pieces of your impressions to assemble as a whole.

It is not my intention to mystify this process. But it is critical that we not impose preconceived schemes or interpretations upon other people. You may have read in a book that red symbolizes anger, but always keep in mind that we humans are complex creatures. Especially where the etheric is involved, it is best to allow the individualized messages of the energy field to reveal themselves to you in their own language and in their own time. This awareness and ability to intuit what is going on comes with experience and, as any energy healer will tell you, "pre-packaged" interpretations of these messages rarely reveal the deeper truths we are seeking.

When we work in the energy field, we encourage energy movement in and around the person we are working on, if we are giving a treatment. Or, if we are doing a personal exercise, we influence the energy movement in and around ourselves. Because that energy movement is very fast, it can be difficult to sense it directly as it moves. It is nonetheless powerful and will create effects which need to be understood. It is, therefore, important to learn to pick up on energy movement *indirectly* by noting the things that happen in the wake of a treatment or exercise. A variety of things relating to the treatment— usually subtle, but not always—can happen over a period of about thirty-six hours, this being the approximate amount of time necessary for the altered energy movement brought about by an energy treatment to sift down to the level of bodily awareness. This is a time period in which we ask those who receive treatments to be on their toes and take note of what happens to them, with the understanding that the treatment will have in some way contributed to what they experience. They are encouraged to note physical reactions, dreams, memories and associations, and allow themselves the necessary time and space for emotional, mental and physical release, which is often also part of the picture. It is not uncommon for a person to want to sleep or spend some time alone after a treatment, and it is good if those needs can be accommodated. Sometimes, even outer events can take on a significant alignment with a person's process, often in the form of so-called coincidences.

I am reminded here of German homeopath Jürgen Becker's organization of phenomena relating to "symptoms"—in the very broadest sense of the word—in five levels. Becker is relating to symptoms which arise in the context of homeopathic practice, but the same applies very nicely to energywork as well. His five levels are:

1. *acute symptoms,* let's say a headache or a sneezing attack, which appear locally (i.e. in a particular part of the body) and arise and subside within a circumscribed period of time;

2. a change in a *chronic condition* which has affected you over a longer period of time;

3. *dreams* which appear in the course of treatment;

4. external occurrences which appear as *coincidences,* external events which you might not otherwise connect with healing processes at all. An example might be a man who has injured his shoulder and is wondering whether or not to go to the doctor for an examination. He is driving in his car on the highway and as he approaches a stretch of road repair, his eye is caught repeatedly by road signs that say, "Shoulder Work Ahead." This sign, which has nothing to do with human shoulders, nonetheless connects with the man's decision process, and he makes a doctor appointment. C.G. Jung called this phenomenon "synchronicity," which he defined as an "acausal relationship." In his book *Memories, Dreams, Reflections* the example he gives is of waking suddenly in the middle of the night with a sudden pain in his head, only to discover that at that exact moment a patient of his, several hundred miles away, put a gun to his head and committed suicide.

5. Then there is the level of the collective or archetypal dimension, which transcends the individual. It is the dimension in which we take part in the greater life of humanity; we understand that we are part of a greater whole. European fairy tales, for example, have such a universal appeal because these perennial stories resonate with the deep, archetypal stories of human existence.

The knowledgeable use of any of the elements that influence the etheric—sound, color, geometry—can call forward responses like this. It is relatively simple in subtle energy therapy, for example, to create a situation in which a person can center themselves—that is, they can shift momentarily to a point of physical, emotional, mental balance— and move into an expanded state of consciousness. This might be experienced as a brief foray, or an extended journey, into a dreamlike state. This can vary widely in degree and intensity from person to person, and from session to session. When that happens, material from other dimensions tends to come into their consciousness. "Other dimensions" can be any dimension that is not your normal waking consciousness. Sometimes people come out of treatments reporting that they were "spoken to" by their body, their higher consciousness, or an angel or guide. One of my computer-savvy clients tells me frequently that he comes into a state in which he can "download" material that had been waiting for him, like e-mail. Most of us relate to this as the process of having an insight, a word I believe we can take quite literally. An in-sight means we have a glimpse into what is going on in our depths. Often, we have to be in a heightened state of energetic balance, which is what the treatment provides, in order to have those insights.

Ironically, some of the contents of the unconscious literally *can't* come to a conscious level without that extra degree of balance. Fear of what might pop up can, in fact, sometimes become a subconscious reason for staying *out* of balance, and this by no means applies only to the fear we typically have of our "dark side." We are used to thinking of "denial" in terms of all the negative things we suspect are lurking under our surfaces. If we are afraid that there is a giant squid or a Moby Dick down there, we certainly aren't going to do anything that decreases the surface tension of the water. But it's not always "suppressed negativity" down in the depths. Conscious use of energywork, for example, can bring up not only our demons and contradictions, but insights into life's subtle connections, sudden clarifications, and the sense of higher guidance which comes when we are in contact with our spiritual qualities. All of this—both our demons and spiritual qualities, shadows and gifts—can create resistance, even in individuals who are "working on themselves."

When we introduce healing elements such as balance, harmony,

> *"Our deepest fear is not that we are inadequate. Our deepest fear is that we are powerful beyond measure."*
>
> MARIANNE WILLIAMSON

sound, color and rhythm into our consciousness, we enliven what is called the physical/etheric interface. By activating this interface, we are inviting an increase in the communication between the various parts of ourselves and between the unconscious and the conscious mind. The sensations and insights that come to us across this threshold, sometimes in unexpected and surprising ways, attest to the infinite variety and richness that is within each of us.

In the relaxation and opening which can result during an energy treatment, the balanced state which arises is curiously nonjudgmental. Previously submerged material comes to mind, feelings and memories arise, no longer held back by the raised eyebrows of our judging minds. When a person experiences this sense of balance—whether through a treatment or an exercise or by some other means—her consciousness is drawn toward a nonpolarized state, that is, a state that is not entangled in the conflicts that usually accompany most of our normal thinking. At this moment we connect with spiritual consciousness where there is no beginning, middle, or end. Not only do categories of good and bad fall away but so do all other paradigms that are perceived as polar. It allows states of consciousness to enter which are completely free of polarities. These nonpolarized states are often associated with wisdom, compassion, love (think of what we mean by "unconditional love"), bliss, and stillness. If we can learn to contact these states, we can do a lot toward alleviating the suffering which comes from being caught in what is called the "Symptom/Misery/Stupidity Cycle" (see the Closing Talk: Progressive Healing at the end of the book).

Healing and the growth of consciousness are inextricably intertwined. There is no healing without some kind of growth in consciousness. And there is no expansion of consciousness without some kind of healing. Since healing is enmeshed with nature's insistence

GRAIN OF SAND

*Think about it:
When you move
a grain of sand
the entire dune
shifts*

*When you gain
an in-sight
your entire life
changes*

ANITA BIRNBERGER

that we grow, this can give rise to the "double whammy" of subtle energywork: repressed material can come up and at the same time there can be the breaking through of higher dimensions of consciousness into our everyday living. When these do break through, change occurs.

In the process of doing energy healing most people begin to notice that their dreams are changing. People who "don't dream," or who say they don't remember their dreams, begin dreaming again. And they remember them more readily. Freud called dreams the "royal road to the unconscious." They can call to our attention issues we have been ignoring. They can depict problems in ways that allow us to see them more clearly than ever before. They can show us stuck patterns of behavior in our lives so that we can be released from them. They can show us what we need to do to make a change and to heal. Memories and recollections can surface. Long-forgotten events can come to mind with great clarity and have an unexpected impact. Likewise, outer events can take place synchronistically which feed the process of our healing and our growing awareness of our lives and our relationships with the world in which we live.

The unconscious material in the etheric comes into motion during a treatment and remains in this state of heightened activation for this day-and-a-half period. It draws our attention to the fact that the contents of the unconscious are in a constant circulation. This means that while certain themes, dominant ideas, blockages, problems move into the foreground of our awareness, others retreat into the background.

Timing is everything and it is not always a good time to work on what we think are our "issues." It is of no use to try and dig around in areas of consciousness that are in retreat; that is, when they are moving with the natural etheric circulation into the background of consciousness. We do ourselves damage when we try to force ourselves into change. This is not to say that we do not need to cultivate healthy discipline, which is always part of setting the stage for change. Change itself, however, comes in its own time and in its own way when we don't try to force or deny the process.

There is such a thing as overzealousness about personal and spiritual development, as well as a kind of fanatical digging around in our psyches that can be so much distraction if it becomes a way of ignoring what is presently in the foreground. Sometimes it's time for a

Woody Allen film. Too often, therapy-oriented people who are "seriously into their spiritual development" want to say a person is "in denial" when actually whatever it is they are supposedly "denying" has simply moved for the time being into the background of their awareness, while something else comes forward spontaneously on its own without having to be forced. It just means that it is time for that to be looked at and dealt with, instead of the supposed "issue."

The etheric, like life, is always in motion. It lives by the motto, "What goes around comes around." It is a soup with everything in it. But we have to accept that sometimes it is the carrots that are swimming by, sometimes the leeks. We have to wait for the potatoes. If we can deal with the carrots and leeks when they bob up, chances are we'll be ready for the potatoes when it's their turn. They'll come soon enough.

II. ETHERIC FLOW

Conscious healing work in your own energy field involves developing your ability to link your awareness with the energy movement around your body. For instance, when we "contact" an energy point, such as our shoulder point, we do it by bringing our attention to the physical area where the point is located and then allowing our attention to be drawn into the energy movement which that point creates. When we do that, the point can become a kind of "intrapsychic portal," that is, we can enter deeper dimensions of consciousness through it. As we have already begun to see in the previous chapters, energy healing includes helping these dimensions to come alive for us, as they relate to our deeper selves. The Basic Etheric Navigation and Sensorium exercises in the first Etheric Laboratory, and the treatments that followed in the second and third Etheric Laboratories, gave us a number of good opportunities to experience the etheric first hand. In this chapter we will add to the experience you have gained from doing those practices.

These energy-active points do not exist all by themselves. They are stable features of an entire field of vibrant energy movement. They are landmarks, so to speak, along a living river of energy that moves around and through our bodies. Think of an actual river that flows to the sea. For all the plant and animal species that depend on it, the river is an artery of life, their habitat and source of their sustenance. The river's health is their health. For humans, it is no different; in addition, the river can also be a means of transportation, communication and even a source of inspiration. In short, a river is an integral part of the ecology it travels through.

Our work here involves learning to navigate the energetic river of life that surrounds our bodies, and this means becoming familiar with its nature and characteristics. No responsible boatsman would undertake a long trip down the Mississippi without first consulting maps and reports by those who have made the trip before him. Likewise, you need to gather together all the information you can about the etheric before you set out to navigate it.

In this chapter, some simple exercises will be introduced which will help you to gain a feel for the way the etheric moves around your body. It is always of benefit to learn the characteristics of this etheric medium since so much of our energy healing work takes place there. We have gotten a good start in the earlier chapters, so before we go any further, let's review what we already know about the etheric:

1. The etheric is the layer of energy which *surrounds and penetrates our bodies* and extends out to about one to one-and-a-half inches from the skin surface.

2. The etheric is the *vibrational bridge* between our physical body and all the other dimensions of energy movement and consciousness which surround us, including aspects of ourselves which are outside of time and space.

3. The etheric is a *storage medium* for the subconscious and of memory.

4. The etheric has *holographic properties,* meaning that no matter where you link with the etheric, you are linking with the whole system.

5. The etheric is *elastic;* you might feel that it is hugged in close to your body in some places, and expanded out well away from the skin surface in others.

6. The etheric *conducts energy and consciousness* and provides the *kinesthetic medium for our senses.*

7. The etheric *reacts to color, sound, rhythm and symbols.*

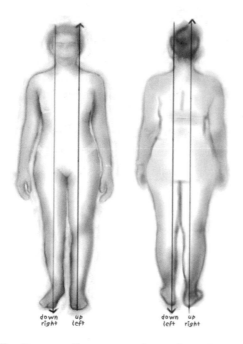

down   up   down   up
right   left   left   right

THE DOMINANT DIRECTIONS OF ETHERIC FLOW—FRONT
AND BACK

That said, I want to add a new property of the etheric; namely, that it has *characteristic patterns of movement.* The dominant or primary direction of etheric flow is up the left front side of the body, and down the back of the left side of the body; up the back of the right side of the body, and down the front of the right side of the body. (It's easier to look at the picture!) This does not mean that there is no movement in the opposite direction, but we are talking here about the *dominant* flow. The most important reason for learning to move with the direction of the etheric is that when we do so, we can support and sometimes accelerate healing processes, while moving against the flow can exacerbate blockages or even create new blockages.

When we look at this situation in the etheric, it is easy to see why chakra rotation behaves the way it does at the etheric level. The chakras are etheric structures, so they rotate according to the etheric flow at that level; that is, up the left side, and down the right.

One of the confusions that arises when comparing different teachings has to do with conflicting ways that energy movement is perceived. The direction of chakra rotation is one example. In Rosalyn Bruyere's well-known book *Wheels of Light: A Study of the Chakras,* (Bon Productions, Arcadia, CA, 1989), chakra rotation is described as clockwise, i.e., in the opposite direction from what is taught here. I believe that at least two factors play a role in these discrepancies. One has to do with the fact that when we move from one layer of the aura to another, we move to the opposite polarity. This means,

DOWN   UP
RIGHT   LEFT

CHAKRA ROTATION follows the dominant direction of etheric movement just off the body; that is, on the right side up the front of the body and down the back, and on the left side of the body, up the back and down the front.

among other things, that an energetic situation showing on the left side of the aura structure, for example, might reflect into the right side of the body. The other concerns one's vantage point; many clairvoyants report that the chakras appear one way when viewed from one level of energy, and a different way when viewed from another.

In my own practice and teaching, I have used the direction outlined in this chapter. It has been my consistent experience that when working at the *etheric* level, i.e. just off the body, we are supporting the dominant movement of the aura at that level. The chakras, being etheric structures, also seem to partake—at the *etheric* level—of that direction of rotation. We have also found that moving against that direction, both internally in personal energy exercises and externally in treatments involving the use of the hands, is comparable to letting a stream of water rush against your open palm. The "stack-up" of water increases its pressure; when it is finally released, it moves with greater force. Briefly moving against the dominant etheric flow can be useful in breaking up and dissolving energy blockage, but for general purposes, I recommend moving with it. Again, going against the flow for a longer time can result in an accentuation of a blockage or even the creation of new blockage.

This is just one of the many examples in energywork of the need to go ahead and have your own experience. Try the exercises the way they are shown and see what your experience is. In what follows, you will find three exercises which emphasize the direction of etheric flow along with some opportunites to reflect on your experience.

ETHERIC FLOW EXERCISE #1:
Going With the Flow

This simple exercise will teach you to direct your attention to the slow river of energy movement around your body. It is a great opportunity to gain more first hand experience of the various attributes of the etheric, and to discover where you have blockage and freedom of energy movement.

EXERCISE STEPS:

1. **Start at the toes on your left foot:** To begin this exercise, bring your awareness to the tips of the toes on your left foot. This is, more

than anything else, a *feeling* contact, because that is the easiest way to link your awareness with the etheric. As the contact deepens, you might feel a change in the sensation at your toes. They might seem to vibrate or change temperature. Go with any change in sensation that might arise and give the contact a minute or so before moving from this position.

2. **Up the left side of your body:** Now move your awareness *on the skin surface* up the front of your left leg and continue up the left side of your body. You might imagine that your awareness is a cool breeze or a gentle hand lightly gliding up the front of your left leg and continuing up the left front side of your body. *Remember that this is a slow, steady movement.* Continue up to the left side of your face and head, over your left ear, then down the back of your head and the back of your body on the left side, down to your foot, ending at your toes.

3. **Repeat this circulation.** Go slowly, but don't dawdle.

4. **End at your toes.**

5. **Switch to the other side of your body:** Disconnect your awareness from the left side and now bring your awareness to your right heel.

6. **Up the back side of your body on the right side:** This time, move the cool breeze or the gentle hand of your awareness up the back side of your right leg and body. Come up the back right side of your head and over your right ear, then move slowly down the right front side of your body, over your toes, along the sole of your right foot to the heel.

7. **Repeat this circulation.** Remember to move slowly and consciously.

8. **End the exercise.** When you have reached your right heel again, linger there for a moment and then disconnect from the exercise.

QUESTIONS:

1. Was your slow movement in the etheric steady and consistent, or were there "snags"—places where you got caught? If so, where?
2. Were there positions where you felt you were drawn either into or out of your body?
3. What, if anything, happened when you moved from the front to the back (or back to front) of your body?

PROJECT: Draw or paint a "map" of your etheric based on what you encountered during the exercise. This is a good way to become aware of the impressions you have picked up in the process of moving this way with the etheric. You can use any materials you have at hand, from colored pencils on a piece of notebook paper to oil paints on canvas, to draw the map of your etheric. If you encountered blockages or patches of different feeling energy, where were they, and how would you depict them? Some people simply color in these areas with a different color. Others find all kinds of imaginative colors and symbols to depict them: a black-handled knife in their back, a golden padlock at their throat, or a dark blue cloud around their left ovary.

Since the etheric is in constant flow and change, this process will yield a snapshot of the time you did the exercise, so this might be interesting to try again in a week or two, so you can note the differences.

WHAT IF I "EXIT" FROM THE EXERCISE?

It is not uncommon, when moving in the etheric like this, to "blank out" for a moment, or find yourself suddenly immersed in thoughts of things far away from the exercise. This tends to happen when you move your awareness through areas of the etheric that contain blockage. Your attention, remember, is a focus of energy and consciousness, and so it activates the etheric, the storehouse of your subconscious, as it moves through. This activation can bring up memories of past experiences. Sometimes, when we move into areas of the etheric in which difficult memories are stored, it is easy to go blank or even fall asleep. This activation of the etheric can also bring about the release of energy that has been trapped in the body or energy field and this, too, can cause a sudden disconnection from the structure of the exercise. These things will happen from time to time, and when they do, don't worry. They are perfectly natural effects of moving your awareness slowly and consciously in the etheric. Your etheric uses this energetic activation as an opportunity for self-healing by releasing excess energy from your body and energy field, and by bringing to mind to what needs your attention.

ETHERIC FLOW EXERCISE #2:
Ten Point Exercise: A Way to Move Deeper Into the Etheric

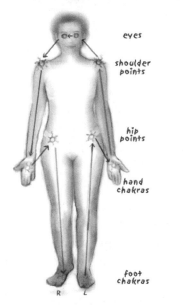

eyes

shoulder
points

hip
points

hand
chakras

foot
chakras

R   L

TEN POINT EXERCISE: This exercise will deepen your contact with ten energy-active positions on the body, and in the process deepen your experience of the etheric.

Here again, we will follow the general etheric circulation and the way it moves on the front of the body—up the left front of the body and down the right front. This time, we will use a number of the energy-active positions we have learned, as well as the dominant direction of the etheric flow. We will also discover that our eyes are energy-active positions.

In this exercise, we will "connect the dots," moving between these landmarks on the river of energy that flows around our body. At each position named in the exercise, we will stop and allow the contact to intensify. This will bring us deeper into the etheric. Pay special attention to the crossover from the left to the right side of the body, which in this exercise takes place at the eyes. Here we go:

EXERCISE STEPS:

1. **Left Foot Chakra:** Bring your awareness to your Left Foot Chakra. This minor chakra is located in the center of the sole of your foot. You contact it the same way as you do any energy-active position: make a feeling contact with the position on the sole of your foot and stay with it about a minute so that the contact can intensify.

2. **Left hip point:** Now move slowly with your awareness up the front of your leg on the skin surface to your left hip point. Again, it can be helpful to imagine a breeze of air, or the light touch of a hand, moving slowly on the skin surface. Pause at the left hip point for a minute, letting the contact deepen.

3. **Left Hand Chakra:** When that contact has been allowed to deepen, move "through the air" to your Left Hand Chakra. This minor chakra

is located in the center of the palm of your hand. Take a minute to allow this contact to build up.

4. **Left shoulder point:** When you have developed a good feeling contact with this position, move your awareness on the skin surface up your arm to your left shoulder point. Again, this is like slowly, consciously stroking the surface of your skin with the paintbrush of your awareness.

5. **Left eye:** When your left shoulder point is activated from about a minute of feeling contact, move on the skin surface up your neck and the side of your face to your left eye. There, make a feeling contact with your entire left eyeball. Stay with this contact for about a minute.

6. **Right eye:** Now move to your right eye and make your feeling contact with your entire right eyeball. Stay with this contact for about a minute.

7. **Right shoulder point:** Now move your awareness down the right side of your face and neck to your right shoulder point. Remember not to "jump," but rather stay on the skin surface. Stay with your feeling contact with the right shoulder point for about a minute.

8. **Right Hand Chakra:** Now move down your arm and make a feeling contact with your Right Hand Chakra. Stay here for a minute or so.

9. **Right hip point:** Move "through the air," this time, to your right hip point. Stay with this feeling contact for a minute or so.

10. **Right Foot Chakra:** Now move your awareness on the skin surface down the front of your leg to your Right Foot Chakra.

11. **Finish the exercise:** When you have spent a minute in a feeling contact with this position, then simply release your focus from any particular position on your body or in your etheric. Take another minute or so to come back to your normal state of mind. This would be a good time to take a few notes on your inner experiences during the exercise.

Here are some questions to help you reflect on your experience:

1. Which positions were easiest for you to contact?
2. Which positions were most difficult for you to contact?
3. What differences, if any, did you feel between the upward and downward movements?
4. What, if anything, happened when you crossed over from the left to the right side of your body at your eyes?

ETHERIC FLOW EXERCISE #3:
Lacing

Can you balance your life force

and embrace the One

without separation?

TAO TE CHING,

LAO TZE

(TRANSLATION BY STANLEY LOMBARDO AND

STEPHEN ADDISS)

Here is another way of "connecting the dots" and moving with your awareness in your energy field. This time you will do it in a way that will allow
the right and left sides of your etheric body to interact more intensely. The
purpose of this exercise is to balance the energies that move through you
and to bring you to a point of stillness and deep meditation.

Be sure you are sitting in a comfortable, upright position. This exercise
takes about twenty-five minutes to complete.

EXERCISE STEPS:

Part One: Moving from one side to the other

1. **Left Foot Chakra:** As in the previous exercise, you begin this exercise by bringing your awareness to your Left Foot Chakra and spending
a minute or so in a feeling contact with this position.

2. **Right knee:** When you have a good contact to your Left Foot
Chakra, move with your awareness to your right knee. Make your feeling contact with the entire knee capsule. Spend a minute allowing this
contact to build.

NOTE: In this exercise, you will notice that you are not always moving your awareness on the skin surface as you were in most of the steps of the previous two exercises. Even though some of these shifts between the positions on the right and left
sides of the body seem to be "jumps," try to make these transitions slowly and consciously. Try to feel what is in the space between the positions as you move among
them.

3. **Left hip point:** Now move your awareness across your body to your left hip point, and allow that contact to build for about a minute.

4. **Right shoulder point:** Now move your awareness across your torso to your right shoulder point. Allow this contact to build for about a minute.

5. **Left side-head point:** Now move your awareness "through" your head to this position located on your skull, two finger-breadths above the top of your left ear and allow this contact to build up for a minute or so.

6. **Right side-head point:** Now move with your awareness "through" the center of your head to arrive at your right side-head point. Let this feeling contact build for a minute.

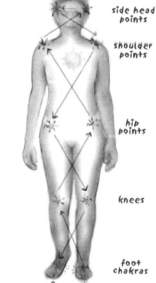

side head points

shoulder points

hip points

knees

foot chakras

R   L

7. **Left shoulder point:** Again, move your awareness though your head and get a feeling contact with your left shoulder point. One minute.

8. **Right hip point:** Move now with your awareness across your body and make contact with your right hip point. One minute.

9. **Left knee:** When you have your contact at the right hip point, move your awareness to your left knee. Remember that the contact is with the entire knee capsule. One minute.

10. **Right Foot Chakra:** Finish part one of the exercise by moving your awareness to your Right Foot Chakra and staying with this feeling contact for a minute.

LACING: This exercise deepens your contact with the etheric and will allow the right and left sides of your etheric body to interact more intensely on an energetic level.

Part Two: Both sides at the same time

1. **Both Foot Chakras at once:** Now take up a feeling contact with both your Right and Left Foot Chakras at the same time. Keep that contact for about a minute and let it intensify.

2. **Both knees at once:** Move now with your awareness up your body to both knees. Stay with this contact for a minute.

3. **Both hip points at once:** Now move with your awareness up your

body to both your right and left hip points. Stay with this contact for a minute.

4. **Both shoulder points at once:** Now move with your awareness up your body to both your right and left shoulder points. Stay with this contact for a minute.

5. **Both side-head points at once:** Now move with your awareness up your body to both your right and left side-head points. Stay with this contact for a minute.

Part Three: Meditation (ten minutes)

Release your contact with your side-head points and bring your awareness into your Heart Chakra. This energy center is located in your upper chest. After you have a feeling contact with your Heart Chakra, in a meditation of about ten minutes, allow any impressions to come forward into your consciousness which want to come. Don't try to censor or judge what comes. Don't try to make anything happen, nor try to prevent anything from happening. Just sit with the experience at hand and let it unfold. Take about ten minutes for this. After ten minutes, come back to your normal state of mind and body feeling. You might want to wiggle your toes and take a few deep breaths or stretch your body as you end your meditation.

Here, again, is the right time to jot down a few notes about your experience.

THE ETHERIC FLOW
EXERCISES AT A GLANCE

ETHERIC FLOW EXERCISE #1:
Going With the Flow

EXERCISE STEPS:
1. Start at the toes on your left foot
2. Up the left side of your body
3. Repeat this circulation
4. End at your toes
5. Switch to the other side of your body
6. Up the back side of your body on the right side
7. Repeat this circulation

ETHERIC FLOW EXERCISE #2:
Ten Point Exercise: A Way to Move Deeper Into the Etheric

EXERCISE STEPS:
1. Left Foot Chakra
2. Left hip point
3. Left Hand Chakra
4. Left shoulder point
5. Left eye
6. Right eye
7. Right shoulder point
8. Right Hand Chakra
9. Right hip point
10. Right Foot Chakra
11. Finish the exercise

⤳

ETHERIC FLOW EXERCISE #3:
Lacing

EXERCISE STEPS:
Part One: Moving from one side to the other
1. Left Foot Chakra
2. Right knee
3. Left hip point
4. Right shoulder point
5. Left side-head point
6. Right side-head point
7. Left shoulder point
8. Right hip point
9. Left knee
10. Right Foot Chakra

Part Two: Both sides at the same time
1. Both Foot Chakras at once
2. Both knees at once
3. Both hip points at once
4. Both shoulder points at once
5. Both side-head points at once

Part Three: Meditation at the Heart Chakra (ten minutes)

FIFTH ETHERIC LABORATORY
Working with the Chakra System

I. The Role of Spirituality
in Energy Healing

IF TWENTY PEOPLE sat in a room to meditate, and the instruction was: "Connect your consciousness with the highest source of life and energy that you know," it is likely that each person in the room would formulate this "source" differently. While one might link with Light, others might link with God, Christ, Buddha, the Universe, the Great Spirit, the Source of Life and Love, or the Oneness of All Being. There would most likely be as many beliefs and names for this source of life as there were people in the room.

The fact is that when we lift our hearts and minds to what we believe to be universal or divine, we also connect with something sacred within ourselves, even if it doesn't match someone else's beliefs. When we make that contact, we bring to the table the best of who we are. That quality of sacredness, however you name it, is indispensable in energy healing.

Subtle energy practices reveal their most essential nature when we recognize that they are spiritual practices, and treat them that way. Though we may never use the word "spiritual" to describe what we are doing, the fact remains that energy-active positions, such as the chakras, are interdimensional portals for our consciousness. Truly linking our consciousness with them will carry us out of our everyday, individualized worlds into contact with forces much larger and more universal than ourselves. As a result, a language that reflects the sacred helps to set the stage for working with the chakras. Not only do the chakras represent aspects of our health and growth in the outer world, but also the many inner pathways that make up the universal spiritual path that we all are on. From this point of view, let me offer some perspectives on the seven primary chakras.

Prayers for an Energyworker Pilgrim[2]

It can be helpful to think of the body as a temple with many doors. Each door is a portal into the mystery of life. The body is alive because of the spirit that inhabits it. Mindfulness of any part will lead to mindfulness of the whole. Mindfulness of the whole will lead to our awareness of the greater mystery.

Each entrance to the temple has its own mystery. Sometimes, I don't know any prayers or invocations to open the door, and still, I am admitted into the temple anyway. I can only guess that a certain state of mind and heart is the essence of all prayers, the master key for opening all doors.

As a conscious being, you enter the entire temple through each door. As a healer you may wish to enter through your hands, as they are the extension, so to speak, of your heart. I like to begin healing sessions with an internal prayer something like this:

Prayer:
God, as my heart is touched by your all-touching spirit, let these hands be blessed as they reach out to touch the world. So let these hands be open. Just as my throat is moved to express the fullness of my heart, so let my hands be able instruments of your love.

---

[2]This section was written while I was on retreat at Shantivanam, near Easton, Kansas, so perhaps I can be forgiven if the title of this section has a more than obvious resonance with *Prayers for a Planetary Pilgrim*, Forest of Peace Books, Easton, KS, 1989, by Fr. Ed Hayes, Shantivanam's former spiritual director.

The bodily temple can be entered through the chakras. Along with a brief perspective on the keys and themes of each chakra, I offer a prayer which you as an energyworker pilgrim may wish to use before entering. Feel free, of course, to create your own prayers or invocations.

ROOT CHAKRA

Prayer:
Creator, lead me to the original ground of my being. Help me to discover my essence beyond reasons, my being beyond purposes, my meaning before you thought of me.

Root Chakra Themes: The Root Chakra is where we gain access to our "root situation." Biologically, our existence in a body, our connection to Earth, and our survival instincts and viability are issues here. In terms of development and our creation of a platform for spiritual life, the Root Chakra reflects groundedness in everyday life, in such aspects as our sense of the geographical place we live, home, livelihood, stability, and sense of direction in this world, as well as our relationship to "gravity," both literally, in the sense of the way our planet encourages us to stay put, and in our sense of finding our own "center of gravity" within ourselves.

The Root Chakra will reflect how we stand in relation to being alive and in a physical body. The Root Chakra facilitates the energetic exchange between ourselves and the planet we live on. This involves virtually every aspect of our lives.

Each chakra has its own rhythm. The Root Chakra's is a relatively slow rhythm when we compare it to the rhythms of the upper chakras. People whose awareness is mostly in their head and in their mental life—whether analytical or intuitive—are often hard put to really make contact with their bodies and the Root Chakra. One of the reasons for this is this chakra's relatively slow rhythm and time sequences. Add to this a bias held by some that "earthly" life is "beneath" the life of the mind or the spirit, and it is possible that awareness of the Root Chakra can recede to the point where its functions are completely unconscious. As a result, what we might call "Root Chakra issues" are often below the threshold of consciousness.

The Root Chakra is, along with the Throat Chakra, critical for personal expression. It seems that being rooted in life, and expression—especially of our spiritual qualities—are intimately connected. A good deal of depression goes back to what might be called a person's "root situation." For concrete manifestations of this, we only need to look at the spiritual and psychological malaise that arises when people lose their home and livelihood. The late Viktor Frankl first developed logotherapy (literally, a therapy oriented toward re-establishing a person's sense of meaningfulness in life) from his experiences among the survivors of World War II concentration camps, people whose root situation—not only home and livelihood, but also family, nationality and identity—had been brutalized and murdered in the starkest imaginable way.

The healing of these issues means gaining a conscious connection with the meaningfulness of mundane, everyday life, the life of the body and—extremely central to healing and development— personal expression. The Root Chakra correlates with many aspects of living, ranging from our ability to survive physically and the degree to which we feel entitled to be here, to our physical and emotional living situation and sources of security and our sense of self-confidence. Basic identity issues are Root Chakra issues. Before questions like "who am I?" can properly be asked, a person has to already be convinced that he or she exists. Many people go for years not totally sure that they exist. They will tell you that they have gone through periods of their lives where they felt invisible, insubstantial. Not as strange as it may sound.

Root Chakra Polarities: On the emotional and psychological level, the Root Chakra reflects themes which organize around the polarities of *success/failure, superiority/inferiority, meaningfulness/meaninglessness.* At one end of the spectrum, survival might be looked upon as "biological success." On the other end, if this polarity is drawn into a deeper, more soulful context, this can relate more to the question of meaning and fulfillment in our lives, the deeper aspect of success.

HARA

Prayer:
Spirit of the Living God, ignite my passion to create living creations, conceived in the dark of night, that can welcome the light of day.

Hara Chakra Themes: Think of a bowl, a vessel that will hold things, if it doesn't leak. Soup bowl, begging bowl, alchemist's cauldron, all of these are useful because they can contain some thing or some process. Through the Hara Chakra we have access to processes of creation which have their home in the bowl of our abdomens. The Hara knows about creation and sexuality, whether in pro-creation of a child or in re-creation of ourselves and our relationship with a significant other. It knows about how we "go pregnant" with creations of all kinds, about luring the seed of inspiration, and about protecting embryonic creations which are still unable to survive on their own.

The Hara is, along with the Pineal Chakra (we'll talk about it soon), part of the circulation of *control*; it relates to emotional control, especially control of anger. Either the Hara Chakra is in good condition and control is natural and effortless, or it is in poor condition and "control" will be an act of will and manipulation of ourselves and probably others, too.

Hara Chakra Polarities: Emotionally and psychologically, the Hara moves back and forth, swinging between being *"in control"* and *"out of control."* As a result, the polarities might be expressed as *"rage"* and *"calm."*

SOLAR PLEXUS

Prayer:
Teach me to turn toward what I fear, and then to open in love.

Solar Plexus Chakra Themes: A healthy chakra, like a flower, is able to open and close. Problems occur when a chakra gets "stuck" and cannot open, or cannot close. The Solar Plexus seems to epitomize this situation because of the kinds of blockages it can develop. These blockages are typically the result of *fear,* which—if it gets out of hand—is the great crippler of all kinds of processes of inner development, the great inhibitor of the expression of our qualities.

There is no way to over-emphasize the importance of healing in the Solar Plexus Chakra. An unhealed Solar Plexus can prevent the coming together of Heaven and Earth within us. Often a person can have an abundant inner life, but because of fears have a terrible time bringing that abundance down to earth by *acting* on it. Fears inhibit the translation of guidance into action, and this always shows in the Solar Plexus Chakra. In the extreme example of a panic attack, because of Solar Plexus blockage (i.e. fear), we get energetically "all balled up" in the center of our body. We enter a state of being cut off from both Heaven and Earth, so to speak. That is to say, we are cut off from the guidance available from higher dimensions of consciousness. At the same time, we "lose our ground," and become cut off from grounding contact with the earth which would ordinarily help us draw that guidance to ourselves.

The Solar Plexus is the first chakra of transmutation, the movement of energy from one state to another. As might be expected, the alchemical element that is active here is fire.

The Solar Plexus, along with the Crown Chakra, is part of the circulation of *balance*. In line with that, the Solar Plexus is a chakra in which imbalances of all sorts can be detected—imbalances of yin and yang, and of structures within us. Disturbances might manifest, for example, in digestive problems, insomnia, sexual dysfunctions, imbalances in pH-levels; that is, acid/alkali levels.

Solar Plexus Chakra Polarities: The polarity reflected here is *love and fear.* This can seem strange at first glance, if we are used to associating love with the heart. But this Solar Plexus polarity refers, in large part, to the way we open ourselves up and close ourselves off to life. Jesus spoke to this polarity when he referred to "perfect love, which casts out all fear." Many psychospiritual systems, notably *A Course in Miracles* and some Buddhist philosophies, say there are only two emotions, "love" and "fear." All other emotions are simply extensions of these.

Many people who become involved with energywork and personal development would like to find some way to tiptoe around the Solar Plexus Chakra, as it often seems to present us with knotholes we have a hard time squeaking through, and black holes that want to

---

GUIDEPOST

When you don't know the next step to take, take the one you are most afraid of

ANITA BIRNBERGER

suck us in. Regardless of what we call our spiritual journey, there are always check points along the way. The Solar Plexus Chakra—alongside all the other roles it plays—can confront us with the terrifying Dweller on the Threshold who scares us half to death. But it also does us the necessary favor of forcing us to gather our strengths—especially our courage. Then, the Dweller on the Threshold becomes our guide.

HEART CHAKRA

Prayer:
Bittersweet the longing of a drop of water for the ocean. Joy and sorrow. Threshold of my body, threshold of my soul.

Heart Chakra Themes: When we closely inspect the colors of light shining through a prism, we see that the middle color is green, the color of the Heart Chakra. The Heart Chakra occupies this middle position among the primary chakras. Looking even more closely at the prismatic color spectrum, we can see that the green, like other colors, has gradations, seven in all: three moving toward white, three toward black, with a balanced "pure" green in the middle. Similarly, the Heart Chakra is a balance point between the upper and lower chakras. It seems also to have the capacity to embrace life in all the forms of experience which these chakras represent.

Again, it is not my intention to re-invent the chakra by reviewing all that has been written about the Heart Chakra and its role in spirituality. Still, there are central Heart Chakra issues which pertain directly to the development of a healer, or anyone who is about the task of consciously developing their spiritual qualities.

Most important, the Heart Chakra allows a spiritual quality to become an *expressed* spiritual quality. Your spiritual qualities will not move outward without the deeper feeling that we call the quality of compassion. When the Heart Chakra opens in compassion for another—whether that "other" is another person, nature, the planet, or even yourself—then it is possible for the energy of your spiritual qualities to move through you.

Heart Chakra Polarities: There is an emotional and psychological double structure reflected in the Heart Chakra; it is *joy and sorrow.*

Though we talk about polarities whenever the true nature of the Heart Chakra is in play, there is, however, also a hint of something just beyond our grasp, something not caught up in polarities. For example, the "Joyful and the Sorrowful Mysteries" of the Rosary are a reference to this quality of the Heart Chakra.

The Heart Chakra brings home strange and diverse characters and has them sit down at the table together. With its capacity to embrace paradox, the heart bridges between opposites and helps them to join and heal. The Heart can go places that the judging mind cannot. It is not for nothing that we speak of finding a "path with heart" when we speak of finding our true calling. Having our heart in something means that we have a deep feeling for what we are doing. The development of our spiritual gifts will put us on that path.

THROAT CHAKRA

Prayer:
God, may I learn to bring forward in silence and sound, a few appropriate words, and through my craft, the rich mystery that you lay on my heart.

Throat Chakra Themes: The Throat Chakra has to do with *expression* in all its various aspects. In the chapter on the characteristics of the etheric, we examined the damage that is incurred when expression is either not allowed to take place, or when that expression is incongruent with our inner reality. This all seems to happen through the Throat Chakra, and the healing of this center will play a direct role in the expression of our real strengths and qualities.

The location of the Throat Chakra tells us a lot about its nature and function. It is situated like a stoplight at a major intersection, regulating traffic flow on the bridge between the head and the body. And that's just the north/south direction of traffic. The cross street of this intersection moves out the shoulders to the arms and hands. Not confined to plane geometry, this traffic of life and energy moves out of the body, and into the inner worlds of consciousness, as well. Located at the intersection itself is, of course, our vocal apparatus, that wonderfully versatile organ which can evoke, invoke, and revoke, express, impress, and repress.

My wife and I were taking a quiet evening walk through a wooded area flanking a residential area of Göppingen, Germany. She was telling me how important it is in therapeutic situations to be able to use the Throat Chakra by using your voice in release of emotion. She also said that it is good protection, if you are ever threatened, to use your voice. To demonstrate, she gave out a bloodcurdling shriek. Immediately, the back lights on the row of houses lit up, dogs went wild and husbands poured out of back doors, still pulling on their jackets. Flashlights in hand, they waded into the woods, combing the vicinity for signs of fresh homicide. We sat on a bench, biting our tongues, feeling terribly embarrassed. Scrupulously honest, all we could say, when asked, was, "We heard it, too." As upsetting as this was for all of us, it certainly demonstrated the power of at least one expression of this chakra.

Together with the Root Chakra, the Throat Chakra is in a circulation of *expression*. It is the strongest chakra of expression because it relates to sound. Since so much of communication takes place through sound, the Throat Chakra also plays a central role in relationships. The flow of life force and information from one place to another inside us is regulated by this interdimensional gatekeeper, the switchboard for communications of all kinds which take place within us, from the distribution of hormones to in-tuition (inner teaching). Bob Moore, a teacher of energywork who lives in Denmark, calls this center "a meeting position between other [higher] dimensions and what we have built up as aspiration, and as such, it is a position of the channeling of intuition."

Throat Chakra Polarities: Not surprisingly, psychological and emotional parallel structures which show in the Throat Chakra tell us much about *expression and repression, holding and release.* These themes wind through all aspects of healing and growth. Ultimately, healing takes us further into *our ability to express spiritual qualities.* Of course, working with the Throat Chakra and its polarities will also teach us much about what keeps us from doing that.

PINEAL CHAKRA

Prayer:
God of Creation, speak to me in the language of light. Open my eyes in this house filled with your countless colors and forms. Seduce my imagi-

nation with the formless contours of your body and align my thoughts, feelings and body with your Light.

Pineal Chakra Themes: The chakra system can be likened to the colors that shine through a prism: Just as light from a single light source is broken up into the seven primary colors through a prism, the life force is divided up into seven chakras when it moves through a living body. If there is a single chakra which most exemplifies this analogy, it is the Pineal Chakra, which *mediates our experience of light on all levels.*

If we were to turn the prismatic process around and follow rays of color backwards, into the prism, we would reach a point where they converge in pure light. Precisely parallel to this, spiritual illumination, in which the physical body becomes infused with spiritual light, greatly accelerating the processes of spiritual growth, is the conscious direct experience of the numinous essence behind all creation. A hallmark of illumination is our realization that the zillions of differentiated forms in creation are unified in this essence, spoken of in Genesis when God said, "Let there be light." (Gen 1:3) This is an available experience; ultimately, all healing and growth of consciousness point in the direction of light.

The Pineal Chakra relates to our potential for clarity, and therefore also to our potential for lack of the same. Of course, the Pineal Chakra doesn't operate in a vacuum; like every other part of our subtle energy system, it is an instrument in a symphony. Its partner among the lower chakras is the Hara Chakra; together they make up what can be called the *circulation of control.* The kinds of trouble we get into when one or the other of these chakras is in an unhealed state are good examples of what this means. The Hara, with its highly emotional nature, for example, is the beautiful focus of the heat and passion of our creative life, but without the "control factor" provided by resonance with the Pineal Chakra, we can become so engrossed in our emotions that there is no room for anything else. At the other end of the spectrum, the insights and guidance—not to mention the experience of light—available at the Pineal Chakra are not of any use, ultimately, unless they can be *grounded.* Furthermore, it is the Pineal's resonance with a healthy and inhabited lower body that makes this possible. Otherwise, we get spaced out, or dissociated.

Pineal Chakra Polarities: Emotionally and psychologically the Pineal Chakra is where we process the polarities of *lightness and darkness, lightness and heaviness.* The phenomenon of Seasonal Affective Disorder (SAD) is testimony to the depressive effects of light deprivation in certain people. Paradoxically, the time of the least physical light at the winter solstice is regarded by many as the high point of the spiritual year, a time when experience of light on the inner planes seems to be more available to more people than at other times. The celebration of the birth of Christ, Hanukkah, the Festival of Lights, the ancient Roman celebration of Saturnalia, and Buddha's Enlightenment Day all coincide, roughly, with the winter solstice.

> *"Lucina": archaic. A midwife. {Lat. goddess of childbirth < lucinus, light-bringing}*
>
> AMERICAN HERITAGE DICTIONARY

LUCINA

What is this ritual?
Solstice is descent
into the densest
point of the dark,
the shortest day,
the longest night,
the nadir of the year. After that,
it's all uphill.

It's the point at which the sun appeared
to ancient astronomers to "stand,"
waiting
for three days and three nights,
like Jesus in the tomb,
at its low point.
The death of light
in this world. Darkness so dark

you braille your way
up the blind alley, the valley
of the shadow.
No light at your feet and no hand
to guide you.
Nothing to do but step
down the unlighted staircase, enter
endarkenment
and feel what the blind feel.

Time drops out. Death sits
in the same dark room with me
behind a brittle veneer.
Dare to breathe and life returns
to the guts,
heart beats out a reminder
that I d o n o t s e e,
but still I am here.
My sentience takes up space,
displaces universe,
has substance that doesn't go away
simply because I forgot my own existence.

Slowly my eyes,
hungry for photons,
collect around them the phosphorus
of some inner life, projecting movies
on the dark screen. But they, too, are shadowed,
winding down, too burdened by their knowing
that they are momentary flickers. They continue to run.
Maybe they wonder
what is next,
when they are finished.

Then black.
This time in earnest. All-absorbing,
embracing and deep. A dive into ebony substance,

luminous darkness.
I relax and new senses are born.
I lean forward.
—JG

❧

CROWN CHAKRA

Prayer:
God of the Universe, open this crown and enter this temple. Join with
Mother Earth in this heart.

Crown Chakra Themes: As we move up the chakra system, we
shift orientation several times in what we mean by "development" as
it applies to healing and the unfolding of spiritual qualities.
Development in one chakra certainly means one thing, and something
else in another. Development in the Root Chakra, among other
things, means organizing a viable, grounded personal identity in a
vital exchange with the Earth and real life. In the Hara Chakra, development entails cultivating control without emotional repression in
order to build a container for the creations we generate. Solar Plexus
Chakra development means a growing ability to face fears and allow
these to become transformative passageways into new openness to life.
Heart Chakra development involves increased capacity for compas-
sionate connection with others, which allows for the movement of the
energy of our spiritual qualities. As the Throat Chakra develops, we
find an increasing congruence between our inner and outer worlds, as
our words and actions come into greater alignment with our evolving
beliefs. As the Pineal Chakra develops, our capacity for conscious
experiences of light, spiritual guidance, and insight becomes greater.

These lower six chakras might be looked upon as "developmental"
chakras because they go through stages of healing and unfoldment as we
grow and become more conscious. The swings of their respective polarities, or parallel structures, characterize their storylines. But what of the
Crown Chakra? It is not a developmental chakra in the same sense as
these others. Instead, it reflects the blend of activity of the other major

chakras and forms a bridge to spirituality, a point of exchange between our consciousness as individuals and the universe. It depends on the activity of the chakras below it. This is typical of the intelligence which manifests in the way the chakras interrelate: the upper chakras, with their capacity for drawing in the inexhaustible energies at large in the universe—the Crown Chakra in particular—wait patiently until the lower chakras are prepared to receive and contain such energies.

The Crown Chakra, along with the Solar Plexus Chakra, is part of the circulation of *balance*. But while the solar plexus reflects the balance, and lack thereof, between the myriads of physiological, emotional and psychological elements at play within us, the Crown Chakra represents the potential that awakens when that balance is struck. Like a white bird hovering over the tip of a perfect pyramid, the Crown Chakra belongs to none of the sides; the Crown Chakra is not involved at all in the battle of polarity.

II. Chakra Healing: Using Elements That Speak the Language of the Etheric

Healing vs. Getting in Touch With vs. Energizing

Though we are seldom used to the idea when we start our exploration of energy healing, our mindful awareness, our intentions, and our capacity for compassion and feeling are our greatest healing tools. Everything we do as healers begins with this; energy healing is about learning to cultivate these capacities and bring them to bear in our work, both with ourselves and with others.

In energy-based healing work, very often "sensing" and "treatment" are indistinguishable. The assumption here is that awareness and attention, of themselves, nudge a process into action that leads to opening, balance, communication within the whole person, and healing. Even when you are merely "getting in touch" with, or locating, a chakra, you are initiating a healing process.

You energize a chakra simply by connecting consciously with it. Remember that this means a *feeling* contact. Think of a neglected child who suddenly starts to receive some simple loving attention. That child blooms and thrives. We all know that it is not really gifts and trust funds that create this change; it's the fact that the child is being attended to by a person who cares. It is the same way with healing in the chakras. We can express it as a simple equation: CARING ATTENTION = ENERGY + CONSCIOUSNESS + FEELING = HEALING POTENTIAL.

The goal of this section is to introduce practices that promote chakra healing by doing things that the etheric, and therefore the chakras, like and respond to. Those things include awareness, sound, color, symbol, expression, control and balance. The idea in these exercises is to create an experiential framework in which these elements can be used as healing tools.

The first part of this section is, at one level, about finding the chakras in your etheric body and making a conscious contact with them. This simple kind of awareness practice invites you to become acquainted with the chakras as specific energy forms. But if you do the exercise by making a *feeling* contact with the chakras, you will see that it is about more than getting an intellectual understanding of where the chakras are located.

The second part of this exercise carries this forward as a healing practice, because it brings together an area of relative weakness with an area of relative strength. In energy healing, we always work on the *communication* between different areas of the energy system. When you move your awareness between an area in the energy system that is strong and one that is weak, or help your treatment partner to do this, you vitalize the weaker area and create more energetic communication throughout the entire system. This is an important piece of healing work.

Locating the Chakras

With this background, let's move now to some practices which put you in direct contact with the energies of the chakras. Of all the various energy-active positions in the etheric body, the seven primary chakras are probably the best known. These seven, the Root, Hara, Solar Plexus, Heart, Throat, Pineal, and Crown Chakras play a major role in the way we process energy. This means they figure in the health and vitality of our physical body, they are active in our mental and emotion life, and are essential to the development of our consciousness.

Since the chakras are situated in the etheric, your approach to contacting them consciously is exactly the same as for any other

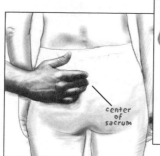

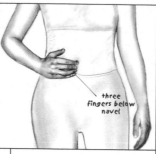

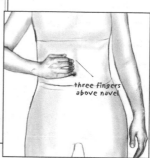

ROOT CHAKRA: A good way to initiate contact with the Root Chakra is to bring your awareness to the center of your sacrum.

HARA CHAKRA: Locate the Hara three finger-breadths beneath your navel.

SOLAR PLEXUS CHAKRA: Locate the Solar Plexus Chakra three finger-breadths above your navel. Remember, this is not the physical solar plexus, which is higher on the body.

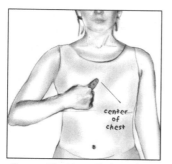

HEART CHAKRA: The Heart Chakra is located in the center of your upper chest.

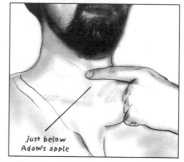

THROAT CHAKRA: Locate the Throat Chakra on the front of your throat, just below your Adam's Apple.

PINEAL CHAKRA: Initiate your contact with the Pineal Chakra three fingers above the bridge of your nose, in the middle of your forehead.

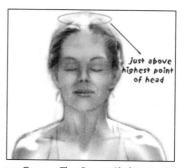

CROWN CHAKRA: The Crown Chakra can be contacted just above the highest point of your head.

LOCATING THE CHAKRAS: Each chakra has a center position. When you are linking your awareness with a chakra, this center position is the best place to start. It is there that the chakra is drawing energy into the body.

energy-active position. Of course, the chakras will have a different feel from that of an energy point, such as the hip point, and each individual chakra will have is own distinctive feel once you truly enter into its energy movement with your awareness.

Chakra Exercise #1:
Basic Chakra Exercise

The purpose of this exercise is to help you consciously contact your chakras in your etheric body. Remember that even this small act of becoming aware of your chakras by linking your consciousness with their energy movement contributes to healing because the chakra will respond to your attention by opening and trying to come into greater balance and energetic communication with the rest of your system.

This will also provide you with experience of the chakra system which you can build on, and it will give you a clear indication of which chakras you can contact easily and which are difficult to feel. You might find that there are chakras that you really enjoy visiting with your awareness, and others that are quite the opposite. Since each chakra relates to themes and issues of health, development and consciousness, this can tip you off to areas of your life that may be asking for attention. Each of these vital energy centers is important, and they all deserve healing and nurture.

Connecting your awareness with the different chakras is a lot like tuning in to a radio station, then turning the dial to tune in to another. When tuning to a radio station, you can tell if you are right on the correct frequency because the signal comes in bright and clear. As you practice with your chakra system, you will find much the same thing happening. At first, it may be difficult to feel you are getting a clear contact, but with practice you will start to have moments of unmistakable contact.

Part 1: Moving Up and Down
(15 minutes = about 1 minute with each position)

In this first part, the idea is to locate the chakra with your senses and spend a minute or so letting the contact with the chakra intensify before moving on to the next one. Even if you do not have a clear and distinct "chakra experience" with each position, don't worry. Trust that the presence of your attention in the vicinity of the chakra will cause some activation. Repeated practice and activation will bring about an eventual "opening" of the chakra on a level that your senses can appreciate. Just like with everything else in life, patience is a good virtue to cultivate in energywork.

Here is a deceptively simple exercise which involves connecting your awareness with each chakra in turn, from bottom to top and then back down again. My suggestion is that you read through all the steps before starting. You will find information on how to locate the chakras as well as some little tips on how to approach this. When you do the exercise, you will pause at each chakra to establish the contact. Here's how you do it:

EXERCISE STEPS:

Upward Movement:

1. **Root Chakra:** The Root Chakra contact is on the center of your tailbone (sacrum). Bring your awareness to this position and feel this area of your body. Try to just let your awareness "hang out" around this position without fixing or concentrating your attention. This gives you the best chance of having your attention drawn into the chakra's energy movement. Allow about a minute for the contact to build up.

2. **Hara Chakra:** From the Root Chakra, travel with your awareness through your body to your contact position for the Hara Chakra, located three finger-breadths under your navel. To locate it, put your index finger in your navel and then place your other fingers under it. Where the tip of your little finger is touching your abdomen is your beginning point. Now remove your finger and make a feeling contact with this position. Again, don't fix your attention on this point; be "loose" with your awareness so that the chakra's energy movement can attract you. Spend about a minute with this contact.

3. **Solar Plexus Chakra:** Now travel up your body on your skin surface to a point three finger-breadths above your navel. Here, you can put the tip of your little finger in your navel and then place your other fingertips on top of it. There, where your index fingertip touches your abdomen is where you start your sensing for the energy of the Solar Plexus Chakra. Remove your finger and with a feeling contact in this area, let yourself be drawn into the activity of the chakra. One minute.

4. **Heart Chakra:** Again, move on the skin surface with your awareness up to the Heart Chakra in the upper center of your chest. The skin surface is always a good beginning place for chakra contact because this is where

the etheric and the physical body come together. Spend a minute here at the Heart Chakra and allow the contact to build up.

5. **Throat Chakra:** From the Heart Chakra, move on the skin surface to the area just under your Adam's apple (is it called the "Eve's apple" on women?). This is the area where it is easiest for your awareness to be drawn into the activity of the Throat Chakra. Go with a feeling contact in this position for about a minute.

6. **Pineal Chakra:** From the Throat Chakra, move your awareness, still on the skin surface, up your face to the center of your forehead. Energetically, this position is sometimes called the "pineal extension position" because it is a good place to be drawn into the movement of the Pineal Chakra. Your feeling contact with the Pineal Chakra can sometimes give you the strong sensation of being drawn either into the center of your head, or out away from your body. Either way, it is part of the typical movement of this chakra. Try to go with it for about a minute.

7. **Crown Chakra:** From the Pineal Chakra, move now to the Crown Chakra. To do this, move your awareness on the skin surface to the crown of your head; that is, the highest point on your head. The easiest place to start your feeling contact with the Crown Chakra is slightly forward from the crown of the head, and slightly up, off the skin surface. This means you are "hovering" with your awareness slightly above the top of your head.

Spend a couple of minutes with this contact, allowing it to intensify.

Downward Movement:

Now we have moved up the chakras, spending a bit of time with each one. Whether you felt a distinct activation or not, each of your chakras is at least a bit more enlivened because you did it. What is more, the activation of each of the lower chakras was brought into the next higher one when you moved into it. For example, when you moved into your Heart Chakra, the new activation you created in the Root, Hara and Solar Plexus Chakras were part of what you "brought with you."

Now we are going to reverse the process and see what happens when we move from activated higher chakras into the lower ones. What makes this not only a way of gaining experience with the chakras, but also a self-healing treatment, is that we are allowing the upper and lower chakras to interact and blend their activity. The lower chakras provide their gift of grounding for the healing vibrations that the upper chakras draw in, so everybody benefits.

1. **Pineal Chakra:** Move now from your Crown Chakra to the "pineal extension point" on your forehead and re-establish your feeling contact with the Pineal Chakra. Give this contact a minute to build up.

2. **Throat Chakra:** Now move back down to your Throat Chakra position just under the Adam's apple. Since you have come to this position from the other direction before, your experience might be very different than the first time. Go with this feeling contact for a minute.

3. **Heart Chakra:** Now move to the Heart Chakra in the middle of your upper chest. Give this contact a minute.

4. **Solar Plexus Chakra:** From the Heart Chakra, move to this position three finger-breadths above your navel and make a feeling contact. One minute.

5. **Hara Chakra:** From the solar plexus, move your awareness on the skin surface to the Hara Chakra contact position three finger-breadths below your navel. One minute.

6. **Root Chakra:** Now you return to where you started this exercise by moving your awareness through your body to the Root Chakra contact position at the center of your tailbone. Allow this feeling contact to build up for about a minute, and then slowly disconnect your contact with the chakra.

Slowly open your eyes, sit for a moment and come back into your normal awareness.

Now is a good time to take a few notes on your experiences with your chakra system. Often, this is a good way to clarify what has just gone on within. Here are some questions to address in your note taking:

1. Which chakras were easy to connect with; that is, which ones did you have immediate contact with?
2. Which ones were more difficult to connect with; which ones produced only faint contact or no contact at all?
3. Did the contact with certain chakras produce physical sensations, images or emotional reactions?
4. Did contact with certain of the chakras take you away from your body?
5. Were you drawn into your body with some of the chakra contacts?

6. What differences did you feel between the upward movement and the downward movement?

Part 2: Chakra Healing Exercise

Now we will take the healing aspect of this chakra exercise one step further by facilitating some communication within your chakra system. If you are like most people, you probably had a chakra or two that were quite easy to feel, while others seemed distant or difficult to find at all, with the others somewhere in between. The point of this next part of the exercise is to set up some interaction between a chakra where you have already got some strength of contact and a chakra where that contact is weak. In doing this, the two chakras will "entrain"; that is, they will come into a stronger alignment and resonance with one another, with the result that the stronger chakra will help the weaker one to become more vital. Here is how you go about it:

EXERCISE STEPS:

1. **Choose two chakras:** Now that you have contacted each chakra in Part 1 of this exercise, choose the chakra that was the *easiest* for you to contact in part one of the exercise, and the one that was the *most difficult* to contact.

2. **Strong Chakra:** Link your awareness first with the chakra that was easiest to contact. Do this exactly the way you did it in Part 1. Allow your feeling contact with this chakra to build up. Stay with it for a good minute.

3. **Weak Chakra:** Now move with your awareness to the other, weaker chakra. You might feel that you are "carrying" the feeling contact you have built up with the stronger chakra with you into the weaker one. Remain in this chakra for a good minute and let this contact intensify.

4. **Back to Strong Chakra:** Now move again to the stronger chakra and allow that contact to grow and deepen. It may feel different this time. Stay a minute in this chakra contact.

5. **Back to Weak Chakra:** Return to the weaker chakra now, letting the contact build for a minute.

6. **Move back and forth:** Move your awareness slowly back and forth between the two chakras a number of times. At each chakra, pause for a minute to let the contact deepen.

7. **Short Meditation:** When you have moved back and forth between these chakras at least three times, sit quietly with both of these chakras in your awareness and allow whatever wants to come forward in your consciousness to do so. Take between five and ten minutes for this part.

8. **End the exercise:** When you are ready, slowly come back to your normal body awareness, and open your eyes. Take down any notes you can about your experience.

Here are a few questions:

1. What happened as these two chakras interacted in this way?
2. Did you perceive changes in the feel of the chakras?
3. Did you find, as you moved back and forth between the two chakras, that you were able to more easily contact the weaker one? Did it "perk up"?
4. Did the stronger chakra change in any way? For example, did your contact with it deepen?
5. What came forward inside you during the short meditation that followed this chakra blending?

Up to now, you have located your chakras in your etheric body and energized them. In noticing the differences between the chakras, you have selected one chakra with which you wanted to do some healing work. You did that by enhancing the communication between this "needy" chakra and a chakra that was already strong. That process has probably already produced some change, but let's take the process further now by exposing that same chakra to elements of consciousness that produce positive change in the etheric. Here is a way to introduce, one by one, some of the healing elements that your chakras will respond to:

CHAKRA EXERCISE #2:
Variable Healing Exercise—Working with Individual Chakras

In self-healing with your chakras, quite often you will be alerted to a chakra that needs your attention. For instance, in the previous exercise, you might have found that one of the chakras was particularly difficult to feel, or you were alerted to it because it was in some way quite different from the others. More indirectly, you might be aware of themes and issues in your life

COLOR	SOUND	ELEMENT	SENSE	EMOTIONAL POLARITIES	CHAKRA	LOCATION	VISUAL GUIDE
Violet					Crown	above highest point of head	
Indigo	"OO"			Lightness / Heaviness	Pineal	3 fingers up from bridge of nose	
Blue	"OH"	Ether	Hearing	Release / Suppression	Throat	below Adams Apple	
Green	"EE"	Air	Touch	Joy / Sorrow	Heart	center of chest	
Yellow	"AY"	Fire	Sight	Love / Fear	Solar Plexus	3 fingers above navel	
Orange	"AaH"	Water	Taste	Calm / Anger	Hara	3 fingers below navel	
Red	"AAH"	Earth	Smell	Success / Failure	Root	center of sacrum	

SYMBOL

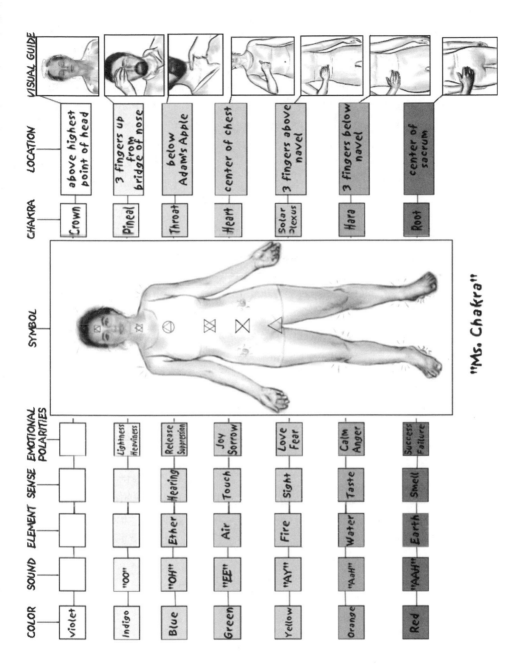

"Ms. Chakra"

MS. CHAKRA'S CHART WITH CHAKRA HEALING ELEMENTS: The etheric, and therefore the chakras, respond to these elements.

that require healing. With the understanding that these themes also relate to aspects of your chakras, you have a means of bringing healing to that aspect in your life by working with the chakra or chakras to which that theme relates. For example, if you find that important relationships are suffering because of a lack of communication, it would be important to work with your Throat Chakra because this energy center relates to themes of sound and expression. It would also be appropriate to work with the "circulation partner" of the Throat Chakra, which is the Root Chakra. We will go into the interesting subject of chakra pairs, and the circulations of energy between them, in the next section on working with the lower chakras.

In order to go beyond a mere intellectual understanding of the issues of communication that might have arisen in your life and relationships, you need to go behind the scenes, so to speak, to the energetic level. This is what chakra work allows you to do. It is at this level where healing and change can enter the picture, something that understanding alone cannot provide.

In order to start the process of energetic change in a chakra, and also gradually in the life themes that that chakra represents, we need to introduce into that chakra elements that it will respond to, according to its nature. The "Ms. Chakra" chart presents elements associated with the healing and development of each chakra.

This next set of exercises and meditations is designed as a structured yet variable way to work with ourselves by addressing each chakra in its own language, so to speak. The language of the chakras is a "dialect" of the language of the etheric, using the basic components of sound, color, symbol and word. In addition to these, each primary chakra, with the exception of the Crown, also has a fundamental parallel structure, or polarity, which provides important keys to the emotional and psychological themes that are accessible when we work with a given chakra. These were discussed in the previous section. Here is a systematic scheme for using color, sound and symbol for exploring and healing the chakras:

EXERCISE STEPS:

1. **Chakra contact:** Choose a chakra with which you want to work. It might be one you feel needs help, or one you simply wish to explore in more depth. Bring your consciousness into the chakra and allow your contact with the chakra to build up. If, for example, you choose the Throat Chakra, you would make your feeling contact with the chakra the same way that you have made contact with it in other exercises. Bring

your awareness into the zone just under your Adam's apple and allow it to be there, with loose and flexible attention. This time, give the chakra a couple of minutes to respond to the presence of your attention and let your contact deepen.

2. **Introduce elements that influence the chakra:** Now that the chakra is activated by your awareness, it is time to introduce one or more of the elements that influence that chakra. These are introduced one at a time.

Choose one or more of the following:

A. **Color:** Visualize the color which corresponds to the chakra and then bring that color into the chakra. In the case of the Throat Chakra, the color you would choose is light blue. Simply visualize the light blue color and introduce it into the chakra. You might create the image of a light blue bandage in your mind's eye and picture that bandage being placed over your Throat Chakra. Once the color is in place, allow it to change in any way it wants to. Don't try to force the color to remain constant. Give this connection a couple of minutes.

B. **Sound:** Sing the vowel sound that corresponds to the chakra. You can, of course, intone it within yourself, but the best way is to sing the vowel sound aloud. It doesn't need to be loud, but when you sing it, let it resonate in your body. The vowel sound for the Throat Chakra is a long "o." "Ohhhhhhhh . . ." Sing this sound vibrantly for a couple of minutes. Feel the effect this has on you.

C. **Symbol:** Visualize the corresponding chakra symbol and bring that symbol into the chakra. For the Throat Chakra, select its symbol from the Ms. Chakra chart. Allow a minute or so to let the chakra respond to the symbol when you have introduced it into the chakra.

3. **Introduce one of the chakra's polarities:** Now that you have activated the chakra by introducing one or more of the above elements into the chakra, it is time to bring in the influence of the chakra's emotional polarity. Choose one word from the pair of opposite aspects associated with that chakra. In our example, this means you would be choosing between "repression" and "expression," or between "holding" and "release," because these words express the polarities associated with the Throat Chakra. It is not the point here to simply repeat the word over and over again, but rather to come into a feeling contact with what that word stands for.

4. **Meditation:** Once you have connected with the feeling behind the word you have chosen, drop the word and remain a while in that feeling. In a short meditation, allow yourself to go along with whatever comes up in you; allow feeling and emotions to come forward. Do not try to analyze what comes. Give yourself 10-15 minutes for this process.

5. **Conclusion:** To end this meditation and exercise, slowly feel your body and breath, maybe wiggle your fingers and toes, and then slowly open your eyes. As with any energy exercise, take some time to regain your sense of your body. After a moment, you might want to get up and dance or move around physically so that your energies can come back into their natural flow.

CHAKRA EXERCISE #3:
Three Polarities (15 minutes)

We are constantly drawing in energy from the universe and from the planet we live on. To put it another way, we live in a constant tension between the polarities that affect us, and one of them is the tension that exists between Heaven and Earth. These two forces meet within us, and express through us. Here are three such polarities that affect us as a result of this tension:

- The Root Chakra sets up the polarity between ourselves and the Earth, as it is our main energetic organ of grounding.
- The Crown Chakra sets up the polarity between ourselves and the universe.
- The Heart Chakra sets up the polarity between ourselves and other people. It is the center through which we develop empathy and compassion, which open the way for our spiritual qualities to express in this world.

THREE POLARITIES: Balance consists of a blend of activity between the three polarities represented by the Root, Heart and Crown Chakras. In this exercise, you create a connection between them.

Balance consists of a blend of activity between these three polarities. It is this balance which allows us to draw in, contain and express higher consciousness. The purpose of this exercise is to create a form which encourages a conscious blending of these three polarities, by bringing them into contact with each other and with a position in the energy field called the Individuality Point, which relates to the spiritual qualities we have developed.

EXERCISE STEPS:

1. **Root Chakra:** This is the same contact that we have used in previous chakra exercises involving the Root Chakra. Make this connection by bringing your awareness to the center of your tailbone. Allow this contact to intensify for a couple of minutes.

2. **Heart Chakra:** Now move your awareness through your body to your Heart Chakra in the center of your upper chest. Give this contact a couple of minutes to build up.

3. **Crown Chakra:** From your Heart Chakra, move up your body to the Crown Chakra just above the crown of your head. Take about two minutes for this contact to deepen.

4. **Individuality point:** When you feel you have good contact with the Crown Chakra, move your awareness slowly upward from your head. Try to get a feeling contact with an area that feels like it is about an arm's length above the crown of your head. This point is called the Individuality Point, or the Transpersonal Point. For most people, finding this position will take some practice, but it is like finding any other energy-active position: when you come into the vicinity, its activity will attract your attention. Because this means moving your awareness well off the body, go slowly, so you won't get disoriented. Give this contact about two minutes.

5. **Crown Chakra:** From the Individuality Point, move slowly back down to the Crown Chakra. Two minutes.

6. **Heart Chakra:** Now move slowly back down your body to reconnect with the Heart Chakra. Two minutes.

7. **Root Chakra:** Move slowly back through your body to the Root Chakra position on your tailbone. Stay with your contact here for two minutes.

8. **End the exercise:** To end the exercise, slowly release your awareness from the Root Chakra and come back to your normal body awareness. Note your experiences.

III. Glory in the Lowest: Re-inhabiting the Lower Chakras

In one of his workshops, Sam Keen told a little story about Martin Luther, who suffered from chronic constipation. Apparently some of his most important work was done while sitting in the privy, waiting for the blessed event. According to Keen, Luther was terribly constipated once and in spite of all his massive efforts to relieve himself, he was miserable. At the same time, he was grappling with fundamental questions of redemption. After much struggle, the flash of realization came to him that it is "not by works that man is redeemed, but by faith and the Grace of God."

In that instant, the strivings at both ends of him joined and his bowels emptied. Glory in the Lowest!

As Above, So Below

The Martin Luther story was told to point out a correspondence between "upper" and "lower" parts of ourselves. While much of traditional western spiritual teaching has tended to hold these apart, preferring to glorify the task of "getting to heaven" and disparage earthly life, the emerging paradigm of spirituality and healing is about the integration of heaven and earth. Every student of spirituality and healing can benefit from a dose of the thinking reflected in the ancient alchemical maxim, "as above, so below." It is a recognition that the same patterns pervade all of creation, no matter on what scale or degree of subtlety. Some of the corollaries of "as above, so below" are:

- "as within, so without"
- "as in the unmanifest, so in the manifest"
- "on Earth as it is in Heaven"
- "as in the macrocosm, so in the microcosm"

This ability to honor all of life, no matter how "high" or "low," implies a growing sensitivity to cosmic life reflected in the nuts and bolts of ordinary everyday life. Hallmarks of that integration might include:

- Comfort with being both spiritual and in a body
- Comfort with being both spiritual and sexual
- Comfort with being spiritual and also able to use power
- Comfort with being a "homeless, nameless wanderer" and having an address on earth, a livelihood and responsibilities
- Comfort with cultivating the monastic dimension of life while living in relationships

Even in systems of spirituality which teach about the energy system and the chakras, the lower chakras (Root, Hara and Solar Plexus) have tended to get short shrift, due to the traditional bias against "the world," and the mistake of equating "the world" with the Earth. On the environmental level, it doesn't take a trained observer to see that the planet is suffering from the effect of neglect and abuse. Energetically, and from the point of view of individual healing, it is often the lower chakras that are suffering, for reasons that are remarkably similar.

This is a common problem among serious spiritual students. Many who involve themselves with the energetics of spiritual growth tend to focus their attention on the upper chakras. For many spiritual seekers, the activation of the higher chakras seems congruent with the notion that spirituality is only about brightness, light and love. Trouble is, all this preoccupation with the upper chakras casts a shadow over the aspects of life embodied in the Root, Hara and Solar Plexus. If a feeling or image associated with those "other" things should arise, the meditator might shove it away because he or she would rather not "give life" to that. Or, if he entertains the thought, or allows the image to enter, he feels guilt afterward. "How could I allow myself to think such impure thoughts?"

The tendency, of course, is to repress such things as aggressive impulses, sexual imagery or possessive thoughts because they do not seem congruent with a spirituality that values only what is "higher." These attitudes, especially when coupled with spiritual practice, do not bode well for the lower chakras, which are then forced to skywrite their plight in dreams of orgies and overflowing toilets.

Grounding and the Physical Body in Spiritual Growth:
The Evolution of Spiritual Practice

One of the most misunderstood aspects of spiritual growth is the role played by the physical body. A spirituality which does not include the body is, by its nature, ungrounded, lacking expression in the everyday world. Without a positive and conscious relationship with the body, we have no means of expressing the energy and intelligence from higher dimensions in a balanced way.

Many members of my father's generation share a common bond in the fact that most of them marched, sailed and flew off to fight World War II. Similarly, I share a bond with that part of my generation which tried hard to "slip the surly bonds of Earth." This was something we accomplished with varying degrees of success, of course, but we shared a common itch to move beyond the expectations and norms of our parents' generation, and not be defined by the limitations of our "conditioning." Most of us merely ended up creating new sets of limitations for ourselves, and still, we had a definite need to break barriers.

There was a time when practically everybody I knew was trying to get real spiritual real fast, willing at the drop of a hat to turn into a sunbeam, an angel or an ascended master, and prepared to do just about anything to accomplish that. Collectively, we swarmed into ashrams and monasteries, crawled up mountains and into caves, attended seminars and retreats guaranteed to "transform" us, got religion and got out of religion, ever stalking the wild vapors of spiritual enlightenment. We ingested secret substances, twirled with the Dervishes and chanted ritual tones for hours and days, trying to reach escape velocity. Now there are many people who have been into fast-track spiritual practices for more than half their lives and are still waiting for their lives to be transformed. Like Icarus in the ancient Greek myth, many members of my generation took off into the sky on wings made of wax. Our initial lift-off was often successful, but as we neared the states we idealized, our beautiful wax wings melted, and we crashed back to Earth. For many, the spiritual lesson is not how to get to Heaven, but how to become grounded and rooted in everyday life.

This zealous attempt to get to Heaven by leaving Earth seems to be a tendency we have inherited from past generations. Down through the ages, many spiritual traditions have been aimed at escaping physical life in favor of getting to Heaven or achieving Nirvana as quickly as possible, circumventing the pain of the flesh. More recently, though, we are seeing a very different need arising in people who are consciously pursuing spiritual development, namely the need to fully come *into* their bodies. We are now in a time when the problem for many spiritual seekers is not getting out of their bodies but rather getting into them. In a certain very significant sense, they are *already* out of their bodies, or, to put it the other way around, they are not completely in their bodies. They are, quite literally, not fully incarnated.

As we've begun to see in these pages, energywork helps us more fully experience our physical bodies. As stated earlier, subtle energy practices relate to the integration of altered states of consciousness into everyday life. They open up the possibility of having genuine experiences of expanded consciousness while remaining in your physical body. In the evolution of spiritual practice, the former "up-and-out" model of spiritual experience gives way to a "ground, center and expand" approach. These concepts, which are now at least part of the vocabulary of meditators, are themselves in a process of evolution.

"Grounding" will not stop referring to the necessity of being rooted in our contact with the Earth, but we need to take this idea beyond the healthful and balancing effects of going barefoot in the garden! In terms of energy, grounding means being fully in our bodies and thereby creating a means of drawing energy and higher consciousness into our everyday lives. Likewise, we need to look at the idea of "centering" not only as a state of balance and mindfulness, but also as what is required in order to naturally expand our consciousness into other dimensions, while at the same time remaining present and in our bodies. Subtle energy practices ought to help us relate more effectively to our everyday lives, to become happier living in these bodies of ours and more vigorous in our relationships and in fulfilling our dreams here on earth.

The membranes that once separated the physical and spiritual worlds have rubbed thin; they are also becoming increasingly semipermeable. We will see a shift away from getting to heaven as the only priority of spiritual people, and an emphasis placed on the work of bringing Heaven and Earth together. One of the insights coming out of bodywork is that a good contact with our bodies—taking care of our bodies, loving our bodies, not being estranged from our bodies, fully inhabiting our bodies—does not contradict spiritual growth. In fact our bodies are essential to spiritual growth. We have to be in our bodies in order to contain, on a conscious level, the transcendent reality that we contact in meditation. We might have extremely deep meditation experiences, but in order for them to be of any use to us in our everyday lives, we have to be able to ground that energy and that consciousness. Our challenge as contemporary mystics and modern spiritual initiates is to bring Heaven and Earth together within ourselves. This is done, in David Abram's phrase, by "accepting the invitation of gravity," in the body and in the prosaic world of jobs, family and community, paying bills and learning to speak the language of the world.

GROUNDING EXERCISE:
Legs, Feet, the Lower Chakras and the Earth Point

The purpose of this exercise is to bring together in one circulation all the elements of grounding. This begins with your lower chakras, those emotional, often misunderstood but thoroughly important energetic organs which, when healthy, keep you rooted like a tree on the planet and in everyday life and still allow you to reach into the heavens with your consciousness. Your legs and feet are brought into the picture in this exercise, as they are, in a vital sense, the extension of your Root Chakra.

In this exercise I will also introduce a new energy-active position, the Earth Point (see the illustration of the exercise). You might want to think of this position as the "South Pole" of your energy field, while the Individuality Point, which was introduced in the previous exercise ("Three Polarities") can be likened to its "North Pole." There will be instructions on how to contact the Earth Point in the exercise. In the process of enhancing the circulation of energy between your lower chakras and your feet and legs, you might have the feeling that you are lowering your center of gravity, or coming down more deeply into your body.

The activation of the lower chakras itself jump-starts the process we typically call "grounding," by increasing your link with the planet. Especially the Root Chakra, which takes in the legs and feet as part of its grounding function. If your Root Chakra is active, it'll enliven your whole Earth connection, because part of what it does is create the polarity between you and the Earth. As you venture "down" into these lower realms of your energy system, feel how you are connected with the wonderful living energy system of this planet which is our home.

This is how you do it:

EXERCISE STEPS:

1. **Solar Plexus Chakra:** Start this exercise by bringing your awareness to the Solar Plexus Chakra. Contact it three finger-breadths above your navel. Remember that "chakra contact" means allowing your awareness to be drawn into the chakra, so keep your attention light, loose and flexible. Remain with this contact for a couple of minutes in order to let it build up.

2. **Hara Chakra:** Move now on the skin surface down to the position three finger-breadths below your navel, which is your contact point for your Hara Chakra. Let this contact build for a couple of minutes.

3. **Root Chakra:** Now move your awareness through your body to the center of your tailbone to make a feeling contact with your Root Chakra. This contact, too, should get a couple of minutes in order to deepen.

4. **Legs and Feet:** From the Root Chakra, move with your awareness slowly down both legs at once. Move your attention on the skin surface of the entire circumference of your legs down to your feet. Continue to move on the skin surface of both your feet and finish at both your Foot Chakras, on the soles of your feet, at once. Remain with this connection to your Foot Chakras for a minute and let it intensify.

5. **Arc on both sides of your body back to Solar Plexus:** Now, from both Foot Chakras at the same time, move your awareness out from the bottoms of your feet in a slow, conscious arc that goes up both sides of your legs and lower body and comes back to the body, connecting at the Solar Plexus Chakra. (See illustration.) When you re-connect with the Solar Plexus Chakra, pause and let your contact deepen.

6. **Repeat the circulation:** Repeat this circulation a number of times,

moving slowly, but consciously, between the Solar Plexus, Hara, and Root Chakras, down both legs to the Foot Chakras, then out away from your body in an arc that then re-connects with the Solar Plexus Chakra. As you repeat this circulation, pause momentarily at each of the chakra positions.

7. **Earth Point:** Your awareness is now at your Solar Plexus Chakra. What you do now is this: move with your awareness slowly downward in a straight line through your body and continue on a line down into the floor below you. If you are standing, this means that you move your awareness straight down to a point below the floor's surface, between your feet. If you are sitting, bring your awareness straight down in a line through your body and continue on from your tailbone to a point below the floor surface. Reach down with your awareness and visualize that you are connecting with energy about one foot below the surface of the floor. We call this the Earth Point.

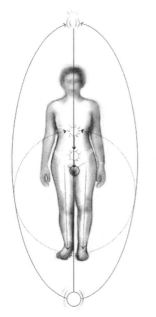

Stay with your awareness in this position for a minute to let this contact build. Extend your awareness far into the Earth below you.

8. **Individuality Point:** Now move with your awareness away from the Earth Point up and around your entire body on all sides in a sweeping arc until you reach the Individuality Point about an arm's length above the crown of your head. Stay here for a minute and allow this contact to intensify.

9. **End at the Root Chakra:** Now move your awareness slowly down from the Individuality Point, through the top of your head and continue down your spine and make contact with your Root Chakra. After letting your contact with the Root Chakra build up here for about a minute, let go of this contact and relax. Allow a bit of time for whatever thoughts, impressions and feelings want to come up in you, then slowly come back to your normal body feeling, open your eyes and end the exercise.

GROUNDING EXERCISE: The purpose of this exercise is to bring together in one circulation all the elements of grounding.

Internal Outreach

The chakras are organs of a unified energy system. They are meant to work together, so if healing is what we're after, we can't pretend that the lower chakras are unimportant. While the upper chakras are geared for drawing in energy, impressions, intelligence from non-physical dimensions of life, the lower chakras, alongside all that they do to stabilize our viability on earth, provide the grounding necessary for containing what the higher chakras draw in.

CIRCULATION EXERCISE:
Blending Upper and Lower Chakras

The purpose of the following chakra exercise is to bring each of the lower chakras into a stronger energetic exchange with its "partner" among the upper chakras. Both members of the pair benefit from this enhanced contact because it gives the upper chakra a means of grounding its energies, while the lower chakra is treated to fresh energies from higher dimensions of consciousness. Here are the pairings:

ROOT CHAKRA AND THROAT CHAKRA: The Circulation of Expression

HARA CHAKRA AND PINEAL CHAKRA: The Circulation of Control

SOLAR PLEXUS CHAKRA AND CROWN CHAKRA: The Circulation of Balance

(Don't worry about the Heart Chakra; it'll show up a bit later.)

Just as the middle C-note on the piano will have a resonance with the other C-notes above it and below it (and—who knows?—it might even send a tingle through that $100 bill in your wallet), the chakras in these pairs have a common resonance, like two octaves of the same musical note. The chakras in these pairs also share common themes, large energetic concerns such as expression, control and balance. A brief discussion of these themes in relation to each of the chakras can be found in Part 1 of this chapter. To recapitulate briefly: the first pair, the Root Chakra and the Throat Chakra, form the circulation of expression; the Hara Chakra and the Pineal Chakra make up the circulation of control; the Solar Plexus Chakra and the Crown

Chakra work together to create the circulation of balance. Expression, control, and balance, and the conditions that prevent these from taking place, are universal themes in energy healing.

The parts of this exercise are presented as a sequence, but they can also be practiced separately.

Part 1: Three Chakra Circulations

EXERCISE STEPS:

Circulation of Expression: Root Chakra and Throat Chakra

1. **Root Chakra:** Bring your awareness to the Root Chakra at the center of your tailbone and allow the contact to build up, allowing about a minute.

2. **Throat Chakra:** Now move with your awareness out away from your body. Feel that you are moving in an arc which sweeps around one side of your body up to your Throat Chakra. Another option is to move your awareness out from your Root Chakra in an arc between your legs, sweeping up the front of your body to your Throat Chakra. After you connect with the Throat Chakra, allow that contact to build up for about a minute.

3. **Root Chakra:** Return by the same route to the Root Chakra and re-establish contact there. Take about a minute for this contact.

4. **Strengthen the connection between these two chakras:** Move back and forth between these two chakras a number of times, allowing the exchange between them to intensify. Each time you connect with one of the chakras of this pair, pause a moment to allow the contact to deepen.

5. End this circulation at your Root Chakra.

6. Consciously disconnect from this chakra pair.

Circulation of Control: Hara Chakra and Pineal Chakra

1. **Hara Chakra:** Move now with your awareness to your Hara Chakra, three finger-breadths below your navel and allow this contact to build for about a minute.

2. **Pineal Chakra:** Now bring your awareness away from your body, into your energy field, and move in a conscious arc up to your Pineal Chakra. Make your contact on your forehead. Let this contact build for a minute.

3. **Strengthen the connection:** Return now to the Hara Chakra by moving in the same arc back to the position below your navel and let that contact build up. Repeat this slow, conscious arcing movement between the Hara and the Throat Chakra a few times, pausing briefly each time you connect your awareness with one of the chakras.

4. End this circulation at your Hara Chakra.

5. Consciously disconnect from this chakra pair.

Circulation of Balance: Solar Plexus Chakra and Crown Chakra

1. **Solar Plexus Chakra:** Move now to your Solar Plexus Chakra. The contact position is located three finger-breadths above your navel. Let this contact deepen for about a minute.

2. **Crown Chakra:** Again, move in an arc out away from your body to your Crown Chakra, just above the crown of your head. Stay with this contact for about a minute.

3. **Strengthen the connection:** Return via the same route to your Solar Plexus and let that contact build up again. Repeat this slow, conscious arc between the two chakras a number of times, pausing at the chakras to let the contact deepen.

4. End this circulation at your Solar Plexus Chakra.

5. Consciously disconnect from this chakra pair.

Part 2: Blending Three Chakra Circulations with the Heart

Now it's time to introduce your Heart Chakra into the blend of upper and lower chakras which we have created in Part 1. Remember that the Heart Chakra is a balance point between the upper and lower chakras. It also brings in the element of compassion, a quality of the Heart Chakra which is able to unite the activity of the spiritual realms with the activity of our everyday lives. Here is how you do it:

EXERCISE STEPS:

1. **Heart Chakra:** First, bring your awareness to your Heart Chakra and allow the contact to build up. Take at least a minute for this contact to deepen.

2. **Root Chakra:** Now bring your awareness out away from your body and move it in an arc around the side of your body to the Root Chakra contact on your tailbone. Allow that contact to build up for a minute.

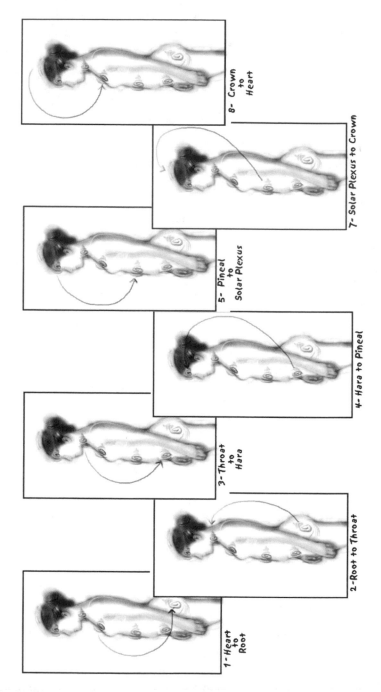

BLENDING THREE CHAKRA CIRCULATIONS WITH THE HEART CHAKRA: These are the individual steps in this exercise which blends the activity of the three chakra circulations.

3. **Throat Chakra:** Move now in an arc around your body to your Throat Chakra on the front of your throat. Allow this contact about a minute to become deeper.

4. **Hara Chakra:** Move your awareness now in an arc down your body to your Hara Chakra. Give this contact about a minute.

5. **Pineal Chakra:** Now move your awareness out away from your body in an arc up to your Pineal Chakra. Let this contact work for about a minute.

6. **Solar Plexus Chakra:** Move now in the same arcing fashion out away from your body to your Solar Plexus Chakra. Allow about a minute for this contact to intensify.

7. **Crown Chakra:** Now move in an arc up to your Crown Chakra and allow about a minute for this contact to build.

8. **Heart Chakra:** Finally, move your awareness in an arc back down to your Heart Chakra. Let this contact be a short meditation, allowing several minutes for whatever impressions, insights and sensations want to come up within you. Take up to ten minutes for this concluding meditation.

9. End the exercise by slowly coming back to your normal body consciousness. Slowly open your eyes and move your body. You might want to take some notes.

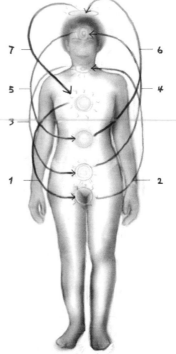

BLENDING THREE CHAKRA CIRCULATIONS WITH THE HEART CHAKRA—Composite of the Exercise

In the exercises of this section, you have worked with grounding in such a way that you not only make yourself more stable, but also in a way that brings your lower chakras into contact with the evolving nature of your spirituality.

THE CHAKRA
EXERCISES AT A GLANCE

CHAKRA EXERCISE #1:
Basic Chakra Exercise

Part 1: Moving Up and Down
(15 minutes = about 1 minute with each position)

EXERCISE STEPS:
   Upward Movement:
   1. Root Chakra
   2. Hara Chakra
   3. Solar Plexus Chakra
   4. Heart Chakra
   5. Throat Chakra
   6. Pineal Chakra
   7. Crown Chakra

   Downward Movement:
   1. Pineal Chakra
   2. Throat Chakra
   3. Heart Chakra
   4. Solar Plexus Chakra
   5. Hara Chakra
   6. Root Chakra

Questions:
   1. Which chakras were easy to connect with; that is, which ones did you have immediate contact with?
   2. Which ones were more difficult to connect with; which ones produced only faint contact or no contact at all?
   3. Did the contact with certain chakras produce physical sensations, images or emotional reactions?
   4. Did contact with certain of the chakras take you away from your body?

5. Were you drawn into your body with some of the chakra contacts?

6. What differences did you feel between the upward movement and the downward movement?

Part 2: Chakra Healing Exercise

EXERCISE STEPS:
1. Choose two chakras
2. Strong Chakra
3. Weak Chakra
4. Back to Strong Chakra
5. Back to the weaker chakra
6. Move back and forth
7. Short meditation
8. End the exercise

─❧

CHAKRA EXERCISE #2:
Variable Healing Exercise: Working with Individual Chakras

EXERCISE STEPS:
1. Chakra contact
2. Introduce elements that influence the chakra
   Choose one or more of the following:
   A. Color
   B. Sound
   C. Symbol
3. Introduce one of the chakra's polarities
4. Meditation
5. Conclusion

─❧

CHAKRA EXERCISE #3:
Three Polarities (15 minutes)

EXERCISE STEPS:
  1. Root Chakra
  2. Heart Chakra
  3. Crown Chakra
  4. Individuality Point
  5. Crown Chakra
  6. Heart Chakra
  7. Root Chakra
  8. End the exercise

∽

GROUNDING EXERCISE:
Legs, Feet , the Lower Chakras and the Earth Point

EXERCISE STEPS:
  1. Solar Plexus Chakra
  2. Hara Chakra
  3. Root Chakra
  4. Legs and Feet
  5. Arc on both sides of your body back to the Solar Plexus
  6. Repeat the circulation
  7. Earth Point
  8. Arc around the body to Individuality Point
  9. End at the Root Chakra

∽

CIRCULATION EXERCISE:
Blending Upper and Lower Chakras

Part 1: Three Chakra Circulations

EXERCISE STEPS:
  Circulation of Expression: Root Chakra and Throat Chakra

1. Root Chakra
2. Throat Chakra
3. Root Chakra
4. Strengthen the connection between these two chakras
5. End this circulation at your Root Chakra

Circulation of Control: Hara Chakra and Pineal Chakra

1. Hara Chakra
2. Pineal Chakra
3. Strengthen the connection by repeating this circulation a few times.
4. End this circulation at your Hara Chakra

Circulation of Balance: Solar Plexus Chakra and Crown Chakra

1. Solar Plexus Chakra
2. Crown Chakra
3. Strengthen the connection by repeating this circulation a few times.
4. End this circulation at your Solar Plexus Chakra

Part 2: Blending three Chakra Circulations with the Heart

EXERCISE STEPS:

1. Heart Chakra
2. Root Chakra
3. Throat Chakra
4. Hara Chakra
5. Pineal Chakra
6. Solar Plexus Chakra
7. Crown Chakra
8. Heart Chakra
9. End the exercise

SIXTH ETHERIC LABORATORY
EXERCISES WITH A RELEASE PHASE

O NE OF THE most important skills to be developed in subtle-energy practice is that of consciously attending to energy movement without trying to make something happen or trying to prevent something from happening. All exercises presented in this book are constructed to reflect the threefold spiritual path of: 1) leaving everyday consciousness, 2) going into an altered state, and then 3) returning to "the world." They allow us to enter some area of experience, and then come back to a normal body awareness and integrate what has been contacted during the process.

Some exercises have a specific "release phase" in which a period of time is included for physical, mental and emotional release, before moving back to physical body awareness or to some structured phase of the exercise. Release can run the gamut from eye fluttering, sighing, a build-up of heat, small twitches, and obvious changes in breathing patterns, to gross motor movements (legs and arms jerking and striking out) and emotional release like crying or laughing. Whether bombastic or very subtle, release is often necessary in order to achieve the kind of balance we need in order to move into deeper states of consciousness that the exercise makes accessible. The ability to move into a release state and back out is a skill which engenders confidence in your inner work. This is a particularly necessary skill if you work with others.

Release also clears the way for fresh impulses to enter. In chakra language, it looks like this: the upper chakras (Heart, Throat, Pineal and Crown) have the job of helping us relate to non-physical dimensions of life. These chakras depend on the healthy functioning of the lower chakras in order to do their job. They relate to higher dimensions of consciousness, but they require the lower chakras for the integration of the intelligence of those higher dimensions into everyday life. In the circulation of energy between the upper and lower chakras, it is often the lower chakras which require a release or clearance of some kind before that circulation can move unimpeded. This is because the lower chakras (Root, Hara and Solar Plexus) process emotional activity quite strongly. Emotional holding and imbalance are probably the major contributors to lack of inspiration (i.e. influx of energy and intelligence from our higher consciousness). Conversely, freedom of movement in the lower chakras and lower body makes it easy for higher energy—and all the interesting things that come with it—to enter in.

It Helps to Be a Little Crazy

Subtle energy practice tends to reveal the images and fantasies that are literally congealed in our flesh—in our bodies, actions, thoughts and memories. Saying yes to healing and inner growth on more than a superficial level can bring a lot to our awareness. It is interesting to note that many of the same defense mechanisms that are in place to protect us from external harm, real or imagined, activated by the sympathetic nervous system in the well-known "fight, freeze or flee" response, do double duty when a person subconsciously feels endangered by what is *within*. Again, we do all kinds of thing to stay out of balance so that what is below the surface *won't* emerge.

Processes of release, clearance and integration are natural and ongoing in healing. It is necessary for us when we are in our role as healers to be comfortable with release of all kinds—both our own and those of the people we work on. It is almost impossible, for example, to accompany another person who is in an emotional release process if we don't trust that dynamic and feel at home with it ourselves. This is a classic example of the need to be intimate with the tools we are using, which also means being comfortable with what happens when we use them. It helps to be a little crazy, therefore, to be at home with what happens when the people we work with fall apart, have their releases, and pass through their knotholes.

Becoming comfortable with emotional release is not the same thing as sticking two fingers down the emotional gullet in order to bring up repressed material by force. There are techniques for forced release, but they are harsh and they can do harm. Early in the human potential movement of the 1970's, a number of methods were developed for bringing about emotional release by forceful means. Invariably, these came with a rhetoric of "elimination;" that is, you had to "get rid of your repressed negativity" by bringing up "your stuff" by any means possible. I think this attitude may have led to the present situation, in which many energyworkers feel obliged to take "negative energy" from the body of the person they are working on and sling it across the room as if they were exorcising demons. I have found that it is generally enough to help that energy to *get moving* again. It knows where to go, and the releases happen by themselves, and much more gently, I might add.

Obviously, if you are sitting on an emotional bomb, the solution is not to go on repressing, but it is better to set up a situation in which release can happen in its own way. What has been repressed—as the word suggests—is under *pressure*. That this restricts the movement of the rest of the energy field is not surprising, resulting in a kind of energetic constipation of other processes as well. Energywork creates a means for a release to come on its own terms, neither repressing nor forcing, and this makes it possible for us to go into what comes *after* the release, and thus complete the process.

Our language is not randomly put together. Words reveal important energetic ideas. "Expression," "impression," "depression," "repression," and "suppression" all tell us something about what we do with our energies. These words tell us about how we hold back expression (re-press) or push down what might be expressed (sup-press), which can lead to a state of holding, in which it is very difficult to express much at all (as in some forms of de-pression). All of these words express energy states quite accurately.

What happens in energywork is that when a degree of balance is restored, even temporarily, there is *movement* in the energy field. The etheric *loosens* and regains some of its natural elastic quality. Expansion occurs. Structures of consciousness which are not in balance are drawn forward into consciousness. Remember that this was repressed material. Long held prisoner, its natural tendency is to try to move toward release (that's what prisoners do). So the instant that the minimum prerequisites are in place—balance, safety, relaxation, openness—the process of transformation and healing starts.

Release of something which is held on the energetic level means that what is released is going from a state of compression to a state of expansion. It is no longer being squeezed together. This de-compression means that the "material" goes into an expansion. It takes up more room. Typically, release—whether physical, mental or emotional—can happen at this stage. Physical release in an energywork session might show subtly in a sigh or change of breathing, twitches or jerks or other spontaneous movement, or not so subtly, as in a shudder or convulsion. The spine can do a quick, hefty release of energy, causing an arm or leg to strike out. For the practitioner, it can feel sometimes like the kind of "pushing hands" practice taught in martial arts in which you learn, probably after being taken by surprise a few times, to offer no resistance to the force coming at you.

Mental release can occur as a flurry of mental images that leave no impact as memories or information. Cartoon images might cavort past the mind's eye to a soundtrack of internal gibberish that goes in one mental ear and out the other, and is gone. This may as well be treated as "just release." Mental images like this can come, for example, when there is a release of energy held in the Solar Plexus Chakra. Change in that chakra is often accompanied by shifts in the mental aura around the head.

Other mental images are definitely not mental release; these are insights, and they have more the character of something coming *into* consciousness, rather than something leaving. The non-physical world, including our own higher consciousness, communicates with our everyday consciousness via symbol, color, sound, archetypal images and intuitive teaching, all vehicles of information or guidance. This can come in split-second blips which have a different feel to them. While the first instance occurs as release of previously held structures, these mental activities signal Pineal Chakra activity which leaves a definite imprint on us and deserves attention.

Stress Level Equalization:
An Energywork Lesson from Tornado Alley

Growing up in Kansas, we had an extra drill at school which children in other parts of the country didn't have. In addition to fire drills and civil defense drills in case of aerial attack on Wichita in those Cold War years, we also had to be shown how to act in case of a tornado.

Over the years, we learned about the weird ways tornadoes behave, and how to adjust our own behavior accordingly. Conventional lore depicted tornadoes as being very capricious about where they land. They move from southwest to northeast and stop politely at rivers. They wad up cars into crumpled balls and pitch them across town, hurl pieces of broom straw through trees, shear off one half of a house, while one foot away a coffee table is left standing with a delicate vase—and flower—completely intact.

One thing people in tornado country take seriously is the fact that these powerful, swirling winds can cause a house to explode if the windows aren't left open.[3] This is because tornadoes generate an extremely low pressure zone. When a concentration of such low pressure comes into close proximity with a closed system of relatively high pressure, such as the air inside a closed-up house, the two pressure zones equalize suddenly, with the result that the house blows up.

ENERGYWORKER TIP: When you give a treatment, take note of what happens when your partner has a release, whether physical or emotional. Be sure to also note what is going on with you around the time when the release takes place. A number of interesting things are at work. One typical kind of physical release occurs—both in energywork and bodywork—with a jerk or a kick of your partner's leg or arm. It can also happen in the lips or lower jaw or in the form of a quivering muscle. These are among the signs that tension is being discharged from the body. Energy which had been held can now move into the general movement of energy around the body.

---

[3] In principle, this is what is *supposed* to happen, but in the case of a tornado, the changes in pressure and force are often too sudden and too extreme, so opening the windows is often not enough to prevent its destruction.

One observable pattern is this: the therapist's tension level drops (i.e. you are giving a treatment and almost "nod off"), while your partner's tension level increases. Remember that in the merging of energy fields that takes place between you and your partner when you give a treatment, the two of you form a single energetic unit. That means that you will tend to balance each other's energy states. Here is a common example: Let's say there is an area of blockage in your partner which is working its way toward a release. The low-pressure zone of the therapist's relaxation sets up a situation in which the relatively high pressure inside your partner will want to move toward an equalization. Suddenly you are jolted back into full wakefulness by a jerk in the body of your partner. When this happens, the therapist's tension level rises sharply, while that of your partner drops.

HEALING EXERCISE WITH A RELEASE PHASE:
Exercise with Two Triangles

This exercise brings together most of the elements you have learned in the course of working through this book, in particular skills you have developed for working in the etheric with energy-active points and chakras, color and the chakra polarities. The specific purpose for this exercise is to provide a safe setting for physical or emotional release, and then a means of integrating what comes to you after the release phase. Release in this context allows healing energy and even insights and guidance from higher dimensions of consciousness to be drawn into your system. This is what makes it a *healing* exercise.

IMPORTANT: No marathons! Be sure to stick to the time limit on the release phase of the exercise. This is an important part of the exercise because it means practicing the skill of both going into and coming out of the release phase with some degree of control. This increases your confidence and sense of safety as you move into what you might otherwise consider to be problem areas, and do some healing work there.

Here is how to do the exercise:

STEP A: Building the Lower Triangle

1. **Left hip point:** Sitting comfortably, bring your awareness to your left hip point, located just inside the curvature of your pelvis on the front

of your body. Sit quietly and feel this point with your awareness. Let it deepen for one minute.

2. **Navel:** Now move with your awareness on the skin surface to your navel. Although we haven't formally introduced the navel as an energy-active position, you will find that it qualifies as one, and an important one, too. Allow a minute for this navel contact to build.

3. **Right hip point:** From your navel, move your awareness now to your right hip point and let this contact intensify for one minute.

4. **Left hip point:** Let your awareness travel on the skin surface back to your left hip point, and allow this contact to deepen for a minute or so.

5. **Retrace the lower triangle:** Now, in order to intensify what you have done, move with your awareness slowly and consciously along the lines of the triangle you have just "drawn" with your awareness on the skin surface of your lower abdomen. Move in the same direction as you did when you created the triangle. Start and end each "lap" of this circulation with your left hip point. Make sure you have good contact with these points. After moving slowly along the lines of the

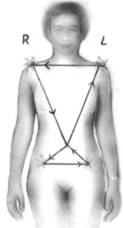

Build the Lower Triangle, starting with the Left Hip Point; Build the Upper Triangle, starting with your Left Shoulder Point.

triangle for a couple of minutes, stop circulating and spend a few moments simply feeling the triangle that has been formed.

STEP B: Building the Upper Triangle

1. **Left shoulder point:** Now that you have used your awareness to create a triangle in the lower part of your body, it's time to do the same thing in the upper part. To do this, bring your awareness to your left shoulder point. It is located at the outer "corner" of your shoulder. Give your shoulder point about a minute to respond to your attention and allow the contact to deepen.

2. **Right shoulder point:** Now move your awareness on the skin surface across your body to your right shoulder point at the "corner" of your right shoulder. Though most people move their attention along

their collarbones, feel free to move your awareness through your neck or along your shoulders behind your neck. Just try to stay on the skin surface. Give the contact with the right shoulder point about a minute.

3. **Navel:** Now move on the skin surface down your body to your navel. Give this contact a minute to build up.

4. **Left shoulder point:** Return now to your left shoulder point by moving your awareness on the skin surface up your body. When you contact this point, give the contact about a minute.

5. **Retrace the upper triangle:** Spend a couple of minutes moving your awareness along the lines of this upper triangle to re-enforce this circulation. Move your awareness along these lines a number of times in the same direction as you moved when you built this triangle, ending with the left shoulder point. Then stop moving your awareness in this circulation and spend a few moments simply feeling this upper-body triangle.

STEP C: Adding a Color

1. **Choose either the upper or lower triangle:** Now that you have established these two triangles, pick one that you would like to work with. When you place a triangle in your energy field in this way, the area inside the triangle is what is affected most directly by the work you do. The lower triangle will therefore involve the Hara Chakra and the upper one will involve the Heart Chakra. It may be that you feel that some healing work is called for with one of them—for example, maybe you felt that the energy in that area was too low or too high—or maybe you would just like to explore. Either way is fine.

2. **Using your breath:** With your awareness in either your Heart Chakra or your Hara Chakra, breathe slowly into that chakra.

3. **Introduce color:** Now visualize in front of you a field of turquoise color, and then "place" the color on the chakra you have chosen. A very good way to do this is to place a Pantone color sheet in your field of vision. (If you can find it, try Pantone #325 turquoise, a specific healing color because of the way it blends green and blue, the colors of the Heart Chakra and the Throat Chakra. Pantone color sheets are available in stores where art supplies are sold.) Look closely at it, and then close your eyes and image that same color within yourself. Now place it on the chakra you have chosen. If you don't have a Pantone color sheet,

simply visualize a lively turquoise color and place it on the chakra. Let it have its effect there for one minute.

NOTE: Do not try to force this color to remain the same after you have placed it on the chakra, because you won't be able to do it. You will find that colors, in general, will shift and change, disappear and fluctuate, maybe even turn black, when they are used like this in your energy field. Especially, it seems, Pantone #325 turquoise. Just allow this to take place, as it is part of the way it interacts with your energy field. Visualize the color, place it on the chakra you chose, and let it do its thing.

I would like to note here that not everyone visualizes color by literally seeing it in their mind's eye. Some people find it difficult to visualize at all, while others expect to see the image they are being asked to visualize as they might see something on TV. Don't be discouraged if it turns out that you are unable to visualize in these ways. It does not mean that you won't be able to do this kind of work.

As with everything else, there is more than one way to skin a cat. What I do is this: when I am doing exercises that involve images and colors like the ones used in these chapters, I put them right in front of me in my field of vision; I place a piece of the Pantone color sheet where I can glance at it momentarily and flash the images into my mind. Some people are kinesthetically oriented, rather than visually, and they have to convert colors and shapes to tactile feelings before they can work with them. If you want to work with a color and find that it doesn't work as a visualization, spread the color sheet out in front of you and touch it with your hands. Close your eyes and feel the radiation of color off the sheet. What you are doing is becoming acquainted with the feel of that specific vibration. Then, when you bring it into the exercise, instead of visualizing the color vibration, simply recall the feeling of that vibration. As you see, there are many ways to go with this, so don't give up.

STEP D: Adding a Chakra Polarity and Entering a Release Phase

1. **Introduce a chakra polarity:** Now that you have chosen a chakra and brought a healing color into it, choose one of the words associated with that chakra's emotional polarities. If you chose the Hara Chakra, the polarities are "anger" and "calm." The polarities for the Heart Chakra are "sorrow" and "joy."

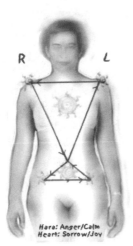

Hara: Anger/Calm
Heart: Sorrow/Joy

Choose either the Heart or the Hara Chakra and add the turquoise color to the triangle that conains the chakra. The chakra's sound can be introduced here (see instructions). Then choose a chakra aspect which belongs with the chakra you have chosen.

The idea here is not to repeat the word over and over, but rather to link with the *feeling* behind the word. This is very important. Get in touch with what that word stands for. It is this feeling contact that will carry you into the theme of the chakra, as well as the issues that need healing.

Allow a couple of minutes for the feeling and energy behind the word you have chosen to have its effect.

2. **Release Period:** Now you have set the stage for a release phase. All the previous steps have set the exercise in motion, so now it is time to disconnect from the feeling of the chakra polarity word and simply pay attention to what is going on inside you.

In a release phase, it is important to allow whatever wants to come up in you spontaneously to do so. This means all physical sensations, emotions, thoughts and images, whether pleasant or unpleasant. Neither force anything to nor prevent anything from happening. Take between ten and fifteen minutes for this. At the end of this period, move to the next step in the exercise.

STEP E: Integration

1. **Left hip point:** You have ended your release phase now, and it is time to work on energetically integrating the experiences which this exercise has opened in you. Move your awareness to your left hip point and allow that contact to build.

2. **Navel:** Now move with your awareness, slowly and consciously along the skin surface to your navel. Pause briefly at your navel before moving on to the next point.

3. **Right shoulder point:** From your navel, move now to your right shoulder point. Pause briefly at your right shoulder point before moving on to the next point.

4. **Left shoulder point:** Move now with your awareness across your body to your left shoulder point. Make a brief contact with this position before moving on to the next point.

5. **Navel:** Now move down your body back to your navel. Make another brief contact with your navel before moving on to the next point.

6. **Right hip point:** From your navel, move your awareness to your right hip point. Pause briefly at this point before moving on to the next point.

7. **Left hip point:** Move now with your awareness back across your body to your left hip point. Finish this circulation here.

8. **End the exercise:** Now that you have completed these steps, come through the release phase, and started an integration of your experience by creating an energy circulation in your etheric body, it is time to slowly and gently close the exercise. Feel your body and your breathing. Slowly open your eyes and stretch your body. After this one, you might want to put on some music and move around a bit.

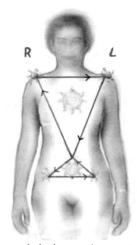

To conclude the exercise, create a circulation which combines both the upper and lower triangles.

THE TWO-TRIANGLE RELEASE
EXERCISE AT A GLANCE

HEALING EXERCISE WITH A RELEASE PHASE:
Exercise with Two Triangles

STEP A: *Building the Lower Triangle*
1. Left hip point
2. Navel
3. Right hip point
4. Left hip point
5. Retrace the lower triangle

STEP B: *Building the Upper Triangle*
1. Left shoulder point
2. Right shoulder point
3. Navel
4. Left shoulder point
5. Retrace the upper triangle

STEP C: *Adding a Color*
1. Choose either the upper or lower triangle
2. Use your breath
3. Introduce color

STEP D: *Adding a Chakra Polarity and Entering a Release Phase*
1. Introduce a chakra polarity
2. Release period

STEP E: *Integration*
1. Left hip point
2. Navel
3. Right shoulder point
4. Left shoulder point
5. Navel

6. **Right hip point**
7. **Left hip point**
8. **End the exercise**

CLOSING TALK
Progressive Healing:
A New Look at Polarity in Healing

A New Place

GROWTH OF CONSCIOUSNESS inevitably takes us beyond what we have established as our everyday reality. It subtly changes our worldview and the way of living our lives that we are most familiar with and propels us beyond boundaries where we previously stopped ourselves. As a result, healing that leads to growth often challenges the notion of "getting back to normal," or returning to the way we were before we started the healing process. By its very nature healing changes our view of reality, hopefully expanding how we experience our lives.

I know a healer named Virgil who I consider to be the genuine article. Virgil comes from Texas and, like it or not, he looks enough like Ronald Reagan to make you wonder if you have come to the right address. Virgil is in his mid-60's and every morning he jumps up and down on his mini-trampoline several hundred times while holding a #5 can of Campbell's Soup out at arm's length in each hand. Try it sometime. Really gets the old ticker into high gear. He says it's better than jogging.

Virgil's healing sessions combine specific breathing techniques along with his own brand of subtle and not-so-subtle bodywork. He has an uncanny ability to track the subtle interior processes within persons who come to him for help. No matter where they are in their process on his healing table, he is right there with them.

I once had the opportunity to assist Virgil in some healing sessions. He begins with an outrageous prayer. Looking around the room like an orator addressing a huge audience, he says something like this: "In this healing, let us all come to a *new place*, one where we haven't ever been before." At this point, the person he is working on swallows audibly, or opens her eyes, and takes a deep breath. For a person coming for the first time for such a treatment, this moment is always a surprise since it is a clear statement that the object of this healing is *not* going to be a return to something which is already known, but rather a move into the unknown. A new place. It is outrageous because Virgil really means it.

From the vantage point of the person lying on Virgil's healing table, these words can be quite unsettling. Here is someone who may have driven across town or even from out of state, and is paying good money for a treatment. She has come in hopes of mellowing out or getting "energized" for an hour, only to hear from this Ronald Reagan look-alike that this healing business has to do with moving into a "new place." The first reaction may be alarm. If she has had some level of experience with healing and personal growth, she may also have an inkling that she will be encountering something from her own subconscious, perhaps shadow material that she had never dealt with until this moment. Just as with going to a new country or trying a brand new experience, people's reactions will vary, from anxiety and resistance to being excited by the prospect of a new discovery.

> *"One does not become enlightened by imagining figures of light, but by making the darkness conscious."*
>
> C.G. JUNG

Most of us have inherited at least a certain degree of our ancestors' fear of the unconscious. This subterranean place within our own consciousness can at first seem dark and forbidding. Freud sought to release us from this fear by providing tools for exploring the human subconscious and demystifying the primitive impulses that so many generations of our ancestors had feared.

If Freud invented psychoanalysis, and saw dream analysis as the doorway to the unconscious, it was his cohort, C.G. Jung, who dared to suggest that the unconscious contained far more than clues to our inhibitions and repressions; it also provided clues to the spiritual dimension of our lives. Jung, who was a student of Oriental and Gnostic philosophy, introduced the idea (in the West) that remarkable wisdom, power and resources are contained in the unconscious or are accessible to us through our dreams and intuition. One of the greatest steps in healing is learning to trust, to say "yes" to these deeper personal processes, which, as we will see, becomes much more than managing symptoms and solving problems and "getting back to normal."

Our friend Virgil's healing sessions were not about getting back to normal so much as they were about peeling back the veil to an expanded view of his client's life. The whole atmosphere around his sessions was charged with the certainty that, more than anything else, the point was to move into a process of growth and change in which we become ever more responsive to life.

Two Modes of Healing

Healing is a natural process, but the reason it is natural is not because we have now decided to take herbal medicines instead of chemical ones, or that we seek the help of an acupuncturist rather than a surgeon. We are each born with self-healing capacities, as is every living organism. And this kind of healing goes on continuously, involving virtually every cell in our body and our whole consciousness. It is a movement—provided by nature—toward re-incorporating parts of ourselves which weren't integrated before. Those who find a way to appreciate that movement and participate in it are often awestruck at how it goes on constantly throughout our whole body and consciousness.

In light of the vastly different healing modes that have developed, I find it helpful to think in terms of "regressive healing" and "progressive healing." These are represented by two different attitudes which are sometimes on speaking terms with one another, but usually are not.

As the words themselves imply, regressive healing focuses on returning to a previous way of being while progressive healing focuses on moving forward.

> Regressive healing:
>   Focuses on returning to
>   previous ways of being.
> Progressive healing:
>   Focuses on moving forward.

Regressive healing refers here to a program of bringing symptoms under control so that the sufferer can make a speedy return to his previous state, that is, to whatever he viewed as "normal." For example, the stressed-out stockbroker goes to his doctor and gets a prescription for high blood pressure medication but returns to the same stressful work environment. By contrast, progressive healing refers to processes that, by their nature, carry us into new ways of being, presumably a way of being that is more in harmony with our inborn, self-healing capacities. For example, our same stockbroker discovers he has high blood pressure, gets medication for it but begins questioning fundamental patterns in his life: why he feels so driven toward financial success, why he chooses to work in a pressure cooker environment that he knows is killing him.

The progressive path is colored by the belief that even our really horrible experiences serve a necessary purpose: our difficulties are part of a process of growth and insight. In fact, what we often find is that some of our most painful experiences were the only way we could have gained access to what we needed to heal in our lives. An example of this kind of progressive healing—a move into a new place—is the following passage from a lecture by German homeopath Jürgen Becker. The case study he refers to was of a Greek woman who had come to him because of a heart condition.

"Things fall apart, so they can 'fall together' at a higher level of order."

MARILYN FERGUSON

I saw her only twice; once when she came for her initial consultation, during which I gave her a single dose of . . . and another about four months later when she back came in order to tell me what had happened.

This was a pious, strictly brought-up Greek Orthodox woman. She was educated, a scholar. She told me that she had experienced a "healing." She told me of two dreams that came in an exact rhythm—14 days after taking her first dose and then 14 days after she took her second dose.

The first dream was this: She encounters a young man, handsome, beautiful even, immaculate, wonderful, her ideal of a man with whom she would fall in love. If she were to encounter such a man in real life, she would immediately say "that is the right man for me, this man and no other."

But he is the Devil. You can't see it by looking at him, no hoofed feet, no horns. He looks perfect, but he's the Devil. She is deeply unsettled by this dream, in which she finds herself falling in love with the Devil.

My impression, again, was that this woman was extremely pious and strictly brought-up, and in her faith there is the idea of Deadly Sin. Once one has committed a Deadly Sin, once you have yielded to fleshly desire— the first time you don't take this rigid, unyielding posture—Deadly Sin immediately enters in and you are damned for all eternity. And so this deep longing of hers for the beautiful young man who is also the Devil is absolutely forbidden, a Deadly Sin. This dream caused a huge upheaval in this woman.

This first dream was not her healing experience, but rather it thrust her into the core of her problem: FEAR OF DEADLY SIN BEFORE GOD ALMIGHTY. If you live in such a state, what kind of image of God do you have? Probably as the kind of God who sits on high, swinging an axe, saying, "Only the one in a hundred, only the one in a thousand who is worthy, will I allow into Heaven. But everyone else gets eternal damnation! You're going to have to take the full consequences of each and every little tiny thing you ever did wrong! Each time you ever had a bad thought— and remember, *God sees everything*—you will pay for each thing! It is hopeless. No matter what you do, no matter how much effort you exert to do everything right. You might succeed in some things but as soon as you make even one little error, you will have to face the full consequences."

And that will go on eternally. No mercy, right? Apparently this woman was confronted with just this in those fourteen days. And then after an exact period, the second dream came: In it, a bright shape made of light comes toward her and she recognizes it as Jesus. Jesus speaks to her very gently, "Hello, Elisabeth." And that was all. This was the healing moment she was talking about.

[Apparently her heart symptoms improved dramatically afterward.] Redemption. It happens like that. There is no way that most of us could possibly produce such an experience in our lives. But *this* woman could. Her inner situation was such that this was what she needed. The form in which it appears makes no difference.

(TRANSLATION BY JG)

I have always found this case history to be a wonderful example of progressive healing. This woman's inner struggle was part of the background of her illness, but it also turned out to be what brought her to the threshold of change. Chemical intervention might have managed to calm her outer symptoms and help her to get back to normal, but it was her dramatic dilemma and its resolution in her dream encounter with Jesus that transported her into something very new indeed. What could be more beautiful?

The Longing of a Drop of Water for the Ocean

What is the "motor" behind progressive healing? The very nature of being alive seems to insist that we grow and that our worlds expand, whether we consciously want that to happen or not! In my work with clients and as a workshop leader, I get to watch the kinds of transformations that come over people when they come, even momentarily, into a state of balance. It seems that when energetic balance is struck within us, we become receptive to fresh impulses that lead us into brand new experiences. The polarity principle, which has special meaning in the striking of that balance, is represented, one way or another, in all approaches to healing. While it is not a complex principle to understand, having a picture of how it works is important.

In its simplest form, a polarity exists anywhere that we establish two points or poles: North and south; left and right; yin and yang; masculine and feminine; positive and negative, etc. When healers set out to understand what is causing a lack of harmony, or dis-ease in a person, they always run into the polarity principle. Whether they are making sure that the right gods are propitiated, yin and yang are balanced, chakras and energy streams are open, vertebrae are aligned, diet is balanced, or pH-levels are properly adjusted, there is an intuitive awareness, at the very least, that balance is essential. The paradox and mystery of spiritually active approaches to healing is that when the natural polarities that influence us come into balance, our consciousness can move completely beyond polarity, and a very different balance, one that is more complete, will enter the picture.

In any healing activity, an ancient and universal spiritual instinct seems to be at work. Healing is at its best, and is the most elegant, when it involves the merest nudge to the system. To use a metaphor, the healer who is adept in subtle healing thinks in terms of giving a nudge to one single log that is the key to freeing the logjam, allowing the stream to flow freely again. At the opposite extreme is the guy who uses dynamite to free the logjam. The stream may flow freely again but in the process the riverbed itself is damaged, creating a whole new set of problems. The healer knows instinctively that imponderably tiny things—the longing of a drop of water for the ocean, a touch or a word or a look of recognition—can tip the soul's scales toward balance and initiate a new cycle.

To test this principle of the power of the imponderably tiny to bring about balance, try this with a pendulum or a small weight on the end of a thread. Get the pendulum swinging, then try to stop its swing by making big movements. To nobody's amazement, the swinging only becomes more violent and out of control. Now try to minimize the swing by concentrating your thoughts on its settling down and becoming still. In no time at all the pendulum will settle down, no longer vacillating between the two poles of its arc.

Progressive healing makes use of the new-found balance resulting from a treatment or a personal exercise to set the stage for the healing energy and new impulses to enter. My favorite personal image for this was given to me by Ruth Pfau, a virtuoso violinist and violist who grew up in Birmingham, Alabama. Ruth has amazing musician's hands: she can open her left hand and make an absolutely straight line from the tip of her index finger to the tip of her thumb. I have heard her play on numerous occasions, and have always been struck with the way she tunes her instrument. She plays double-stops: two strings are played together simultaneously while she tunes them with the tuning pegs. (This may be how they all do it, but it was new to me.) When the strings are perfectly in tune, the sounds of the two strings seem to blend and automatically a *third note,* a pure crystalline overtone, appears, as if from nowhere. She waits for that overtone as a signal that the strings are in tune. Once, she noticed my delight when that happened, and said, "Wherever two or more are gathered . . ., there am I!"

It seems that other dimensions—in the case of Ruth's viola, the overtones—are already there, waiting in the wings until conditions are right. Beside the sheer pleasure of hearing Ruth play, my delight came from an insight: when the overtone sounded, clear and bright, I had the thought, "That's exactly how energy healing works!" Though it applies to energywork in general, I was thinking in particular about polarity energy-balancing therapy, in which we place our hands on pairs of energy-active positions—"polarity positions"—on either side of the body. Then we simply allow the energetic exchange between our hands to take place. In time, the energetic system of the person receiving the treatment will naturally shift into a balanced state, and this brings with it a host of effects including the release of tension, relaxation, energization, faster recovery from injuries and diseases.

But the question that kept me busy was: Why do people also regularly experience flashes of insight during treatments, and an infusion of new energy which seems to carry them forward in their lives? I already knew that polarity treatments and energywork helped people to move more easily into meditative states, but Ruth and her overtones gave me an important clue about the dynamic of this process of progressive healing.

Polarity treatments make use of what I have called energy-active positions on the body. As we learned in the lessons on subtle anatomy and in the Elementary Polarity Treatment Protocol, these energy positions are active in the energy field and their activity penetrates the physical body. I made the point earlier that the energy field, and in particular the layer we call the etheric, is the storehouse of the subconscious and an energetic link between the body and the psyche. In polarity treatments, we are enlivening and bringing balance to the place where the body and the psyche meet. The result can be a sense of tapping into wisdom both personal and beyond the personal.

Your partner may experience this moment of connecting the polarities as a deep sense of relaxation, or a release from tension or pain, or an insight into something that had previously been a mystery or source of conflict for them. In the blend that occurs, there may be a new synthesis, such as a new way of looking at an old problem or conflict.

For example, a woman, Julia, who had recently married, was in a conflict about whether or not she was ready to have children. Her husband grew up in a culture where it was expected that they would start a family immediately. Julia's new family situation created a lot of pressure for her because she no longer felt free to make her own decision on this important issue. During a polarity session to release tension in her back and shoulders, her whole body suddenly relaxed. She wept with relief as a new insight broke through in the process. She realized that her own mother had been extremely ambivalent about having children when she was in her early 20's and had bowed to external pressure to do so. In the process of the polarity release Julia not only released her body tension,

> *"In Christ there is no East or West,*
> *In Him no North or South."*
>
> CHRISTIAN HYMN

but also understood that she had been given an "assignment" to learn to do something that her mother had never learned to do, namely, make sure that if there were to be children, it would be at a time of her own choosing.

What's important to recognize in polarity work is that the apparent facts about a source of tension or discomfort don't necessarily change. For example, Julia's husband and his Latino family didn't suddenly change their attitudes about a woman's say in having babies. But now, through the connection and synthesis of the poles within her, something new was created in Julia, a flash of insight arose and a potential that was always there moved to the forefront. Julia's balance and insight opened her to something new about her *own* strengths and potential to resolve her conflict.

A person's life can change in a heartbeat. Just as with meditation and prayer, the polarity process in energywork can:

- invoke Heaven
- call in energy from other dimensions
- invite insight
- create that "3rd point" that changes everything
- ignite the creative process

Constellation

Five hundred years ago, Renaissance philosopher Marsilio Ficino described illness as a form of "monotheism," that is to say, a person's life comes to be dominated by one god, their imagination fixed in a single kind of consciousness. Ficino's examples included ailments, expressed in astrological language, such as depression (a domination of Saturn), obsession with relationship and sexuality (a domination of Venus), and choleric aggressiveness (a domination of Mars). Nowadays we might say that a person is "stuck" or "hung up," has neuroses, fixations, obsessions, is living a kind of one-sidedness, is out of balance. Ficino's idea was to find a way to offset the one-sided tendency by inviting in an opposite kind of spirit, while at the same time experiencing the dominant spirit in great depth. He prescribed a whole array of "remedies," including specific activities, foods, wines, objects of contemplation, music, sex, and contact with nature—not as an attempt to repress or get rid of the problem (or dominant spirit, in Ficino's terms) but rather to invite a healthful *constellation of influences* in that person's life. This creates the kind of envi-

> *"Regardless of the subject, balance comes only when both sides are given their due."*
>
> ROBERT A. JOHNSON

> *"It is our lot, if we are honest, to live in duality and paradox. The dialogue of those paradoxical elements is the stuff of life. Surprisingly, it is also the surest path toward unity."*
>
> ROBERT A. JOHNSON

ronment which the soul needs in order to balance and heal itself, and continue its progress.

Ficino obviously sensed that the tension between natural polarities—all the different conjugations of masculine and feminine—is the medium for healing, and, with the restoration of that tension, its close relative, creativity. For when male and female interact, they create, whether literal physical offspring, the million objects and activities that our wishes and thoughts give rise to, or a means of moving into other dimensions of consciousness. Male and female can only be separated on a physical level. If we try to keep them apart, we eliminate the means by which we can experience what is beyond the physical.

> *"Many men are scared of women and many women are scared of men, {but} what they are actually scared of is themselves. These polarities exist within us and what we are scared of is what these polarities create."*
>
> BOB MOORE

The most basic and inherent spirituality of energywork rises out of its capacity for creating meaningful constellations of the forces that act on us. Energywork, in particular the polarity-type treatment, becomes an art of skillful placement, a *feng shui* of the inner world. Though very simple, it can be one of the most important tools in a healer's bag because it offers an opportunity for a subtle kind of Ficinian constellation. When this type of treatment is used with some understanding of how to find and make good contact with the polarity positions, and when it is done with a decent amount of care and consciousness, the results are often quite impressive.

> *"An idea or an insight doesn't come from a single happening, it requires a meeting to alter perspective. Often it takes a while for the events to collide, but when they do it is inevitable that a change will follow."*
>
> NICK BANTOCK

Polarity and energy-balancing exercises and treatments are effective because they address—literally and figuratively—*both sides* of a person. Polarity positions on the body and areas of holding (physical, emotional, mental and energetic) relax and expand when allowed to interact with their counterparts of the opposite polarity. Emotional release is not uncommon in treatments; what has been held now has a way to move. Undercharged zones draw energy and new life to themselves, and the whole system relaxes and expands. All this relaxation and mobilization of energy guides the system toward release and shift of consciousness to what is beyond polarities, and here, something very important happens. We take a quantum leap out of the ruts we have been caught in.

Breaking out of the "Symptom/Misery/Stupidity Cycle"

The "monotheistic stuckness" described by Ficino is a repetitious pattern like what psychologists John Dollard and Niel Miller, in their reformulation of the Freudian concept of neurosis, called the "Symptom/Misery/Stupidity Cycle." Symptoms, and the misery they cause, cycle again and again because there is, at the same time, a shutting down of what Dollard and Miller refer to as "higher thought processes." This shutting down is the "stupidity" part of the cycle: without the intelligence and fresh impulses from higher dimensions of consciousness, usually in the form of what we call "catching on," or having the "light go on in our head," we literally don't know what to do. As a result, we tend to fall back on what we have done in the past and make the same mistakes over and over again, perpetuating the cycle. Graphically, it looks like this:

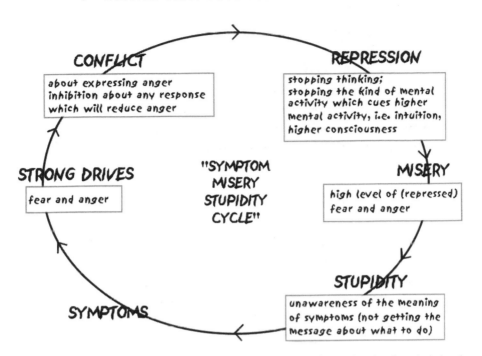

SYMPTOM/MISERY/STUPIDITY CYCLE: This is how psychologists John Dollard and Niel Miller reformulated the Freudian concept of neurosis.

Dollard and Miller's explanation of the "Symptom/Misery/Stupidity Cycle" begins with the repression ("repressed expression"—JG) of a strong drive, such as that of an emotion like anger or fear. Let's say a child is angry at his parents, but has real reasons to fear the consequences of expressing the anger. Odds are against the kid in a fight, so self-preservation means repression. The expression of the anger is shut down, but the anger is still there, of course. It goes underground where it creates anxiety in one form or another. We have the tendency to do things that reduce anxiety, and generally, the reduction of anxiety and tension feels good, so we do them. But if this means further repressing the anger (which caused the anxiety in the first place), then the thing that is done to reduce the tension is continued as a neurotic symptom and is difficult to give up.

Energy healing practices which succeed in balancing our polarities interrupt the Symptom/Misery/Stupidity Cycle. They set us up for an influx of energy and intelligence from a transcendent level of life which is not caught up with our problems. This type of transcendent experience has the potential to break us out of ruts because it emanates from dimensions of life which are not on the level of the problem. This is basically what is meant by the "strengths perspective," which says that we are barking up the wrong tree when we try to solve a problem on the level of the problem. It is better to go to an area of strength, and approach the problem from there. If you are in balance, and can operate from a position of strength—even for a short time—you have a better chance of affecting change than if you remain stuck in the Symptom/Misery/Stupidity Cycle. Remember Julia's process: instead of trying to make her husband change his attitudes, she found a source of motivation and the inner strength to take her situation in hand.

Often, it is necessary, as Ron Kurtz puts it, to "jump out of the system": we have to move to an area of strength before we will be able to truly heal what ails us. The source of that strength is what our souls are longing for anyway, it seems. So our "problems" may some day be recognized as the very ox goads that help us to go where we always wanted to go.

Healing, in all its more eloquent forms, sets the stage for inspiration to enter our experience. Something new is born. It is this influx of spirit, the breaking through of life from a bigger world, that gives us renewable chances, not only to break free of the "Symptom/Misery/Stupidity Cycle," but also to find ourselves, express our gifts.

This journey of transformation—from problems to exploration to experience of transcendent realities—is what progressive healing is all about. The polarities at work in our bodies and psyches create all kinds of conflicts when they are out of balance. Once in a healing balance, however, they provide fertile ground for our inner growth and draw to us what we need in order to be more sure-footed and confident as we find our way home.

AFTERWORD

THE FOREGOING PRACTICES have been offered in the same spirit in which one offers tools to an artisan—if you already have your own chisel, then you don't need mine. In other cases, they are like comparing maps among fellow travelers who want to explore the same territory—your map may show details that my map doesn't, and vice-versa. Most often, however, these exercises seem like recipes. Some of them I have learned from others and elaborated upon from my own experience. Others I have concocted myself. In each of them, I have tried to pass on a whole protein. Energywork has many ingredients, and as recipes these practices suggest ways of putting those ingredients together. But, as Ed Espe Brown said in his wonderful, spiritual book, *The Tassajara Bread Book,* the bread bakes itself. May these recipes nourish you. May your skills as a healer increase. I have a feeling you are going to be needed.

Like anything you take the time to learn and put your heart into, energy healing is a source of joy.

"Bread makes itself, by your kindness, with your help, with imagination running through you, with dough under hand, you are breadmaking itself, which is why breadmaking is so fulfilling and rewarding.

A recipe doesn't belong to anyone. Given to me, I give it to you. Only a guide, only a skeletal framework. You must fill in the flesh according to your nature and desire. Your life, your love will bring these words into full creation. This cannot be taught. You already know. So please cook, love, feel, create."

ED ESPE BROWN

GLOSSARY OF TERMS

CENTERING: the process of coming into energetic balance or equilibrium

CHAKRA: Sanskrit for "wheel"; vortices of energy movement located in the etheric; these etheric structures are stable features of the human energy field which play a major energetic role in all aspects of human growth and development

CHAKRA PAIR: a lower and an upper chakra which are part of the same resonance or circulation of energy; these pairs are the Root Chakra and Throat Chakra, which make up the Circulation of Expression; the Hara Chakra and Pineal Chakra which make up the the Circulation of Control; and the Solar Plexus Chakra and Crown Chakra which make up the the Circulation of Balance

CHAKRA POLARITIES: the emotional or functional polarities associated with most chakras; these are used in chakra healing exercises for bringing about release and balance

EARTH POINT: the "South Pole" of the human energy field; associated with an individual's grounding and connection with the planet

ENERGY CYST: localized, encapsulated zones of disorganized energy. Typically, an energy cyst forms in the energy field when there is trauma and injury

ENERGY POINT: energy-active positions in the etheric; stable features of the human energy field

ENERGYWORK: the knowledgeable and purposeful use, whether by individuals or groups, of the energy field that surrounds and penetrates the human body for healing and growth of consciousness

ETHERIC: the layers of the energy field which immediately surround and penetrate the physical body; also called the "vital aura" or "health aura"

ETHERIC CIRCULATION: the movement of the energy of the etheric
around the body; the movement of the contents of the etheric, such
as memory

GROUNDING: the process by which we connect energetically with the
Earth and with everyday life

HOLOGRAPHY: the theory that each of the smallest units of energy,
light, or matter embody an understanding of the whole

INDIVIDUALITY POINT: the "North Pole" of the human energy field;
associated with an individual's transpersonal aspect or soul; also
referred to as the "transpersonal point"

NADI: subtle energetic filaments which play a role in the transformation of energy as it enters our physical/energetic system; the nadis
are the subtle energetic counterparts of the nervous system

PARASYMPATHETIC NERVOUS SYSTEM: the aspect of the autonomic
nervous system which enables us to return to normal function after
an episode of excitement or danger

POLARITY POINT: one of a set of paired energy-active positions in the
etheric body which relate to balance in the human energy system

POLARITY THERAPY: a form of subtle energy therapy, developed by
Dr. Randolph Stone, in which the hands are used to restore energetic balance to the body/mind system; also called "energy balancing"

PRANA: Sanskrit for "life-force"

PROGRESSIVE HEALING: healing which focuses on moving forward,
into new ways of being

REGRESSIVE HEALING: healing which focuses on returning to previous
ways of being

SENSORIUM: the entire arena of our senses

SYMPATHETIC NERVOUS SYSTEM: the aspect of the autonomic nervous
system which is the mechanism for the "fight or flight" response

SYMPTOM/MISERY/STUPIDITY CYCLE: a term coined by psychologists
John Dollard and Niel Miller, referring to symptoms, and the misery they cause, which cycle again and again because there is, at the
same time, a shutting down of what they refer to as "higher
thought processes"

BIBLIOGRAPHY

Abram, David, *The Spell of the Sensuous,* Random House, Inc., New York, 1996.

Artress, Lauren, *Walking a Spiritual Path: Rediscovering the Labyrinth as a Spiritual Tool,* Riverhead Books, New York, 1995.

Becker, Jürgen, "Ferrum phosphoricum (Iron Phosphate)" from *Homeopathic Remedies in Research and Practice, or How the Living Essences of the Material World can Cause and Heal Illness,* unpublished manuscript, translated by James Gilkeson.

——, Lecture on arsenicum album, *Homöopathiewoche,* Bad Boll, Germany, translated by James Gilkeson.

Becker, Sonja, lecture on natrium muriaticum, *Homöopathiewoche,* Bad Boll, Germany, translated by James Gilkeson.

Birnberger, Anita, *Einsichten,* Selbstverlag, Deggendorf, Germany, 1994 (translated by James Gilkeson).

Brown, Ed Espe, *Tassajara Bread Book,* The Chief Priest, Zen Center, San Francisco, 1970.

Bruyere, Rosalyn, *Wheels of Light: A Study of the Chakras,* Bon Productions, Arcadia, CA, 1989

Campbell, Joseph, *The Hero with a Thousand Faces,* Bollingen Foundation, Inc., Princeton University Press, Princeton, NJ, 1949.

Dollard John, *Frustration and Aggression,* Greenwood Publishing Group, 1980.

Dossey, Larry, "The Forces of Healing: Reflections on Energy, Consciousness and the Beef Stroganoff Principle," *Alternative Therapies in Health and Medicine,* September, 1997.

Einstein, Albert. Quoted by Pirsig, Robert in *Zen and the Art of Motorcycle Maintenance,* Wm. Morrow, 1974.

Ferguson, Marilyn, *Radical Science—The Emerging Paradigm and the Wavy World*, Lecture, ISSSEEM Conference, Boulder, CO, 1996.

Frankl, Viktor E., *Man's Search for Meaning: An Introduction to Logotherapy*, 3rd Edition, Simon and Schuster, New York, 1984.

Galanter, E., *Contemporary Psychophysics*, In R. Brown, E. Galanter, E. H. Hess, & G. Mandler (Eds.), *New Directions in Psychology*, New York: Holt, Rinehart & Winston, 1962.

Gerber, Richard, *Vibrational Medicine: New Choices for Healing Ourselves,* Bear & Company, Santa Fe, 1988.

Gordon, Richard, *Your Healing Hands: The Polarity Experience,* Wingbow Press, 1984.

Hayes, Edward M., *Prayers for a Planetary Pilgrim*, Forest of Peace Books, Easton, KS, 1989.

Johnson, Robert A., *Inner Work,* Harper & Row, New York, 1986.

Juhan, Deane, *Job's Body: A Handbook for Bodywork,* Station Hill Press, Inc., Barrytown, New York, 1987.

Jung, Carl, *Memories, Dreams and Recollections,* reissued edition, Vintage Books, 1989.

Kahn, Pir Vilayat, *Introducing Spirituality into Counseling and Therapy,* Omega Press, Santa Fe, New Mexico, 1982.

Kurtz, Ron, *Body-Centered Psychotherapy: The Hakomi Method,* LifeRhythm, Mendocino, CA, 1990.

——, and Greg Johanson, *Grace Unfolding: Psychotherapy in the Spirit of the Tao-te Ching*, Harmony Books, 1994.

Lao Tze, *Tao te Ching,* Lombardo, Stanley and Addiss, Stephen (translators), Hackett Publishing Co., Indianapolis, IN, 1993.

Lewis, Samuel, *This is the New Age, in Person*, Omen Press, 1973.

Marti, Ernst, *The Four Ethers: Contributions to Rudolf Steiner's Science of the Ethers, Elements-Ethers-Formative Forces,* Schaumburg Publications.

Miller, Neal E. and John Dollard, *Social Learning and Imitation*, Greenwood Publishing Group, 1979.

Milner, D.R., *The Loom of Creation*, Neville Spearman, Ltd., 1976.

Moore, Bob, *Conversations with Bob Moore*, Anna and Alexander Mauthner (publishers), Kirchdorf, Switzerland, 1992.

Moore, Thomas, *The Planets Within,* Lindesfarne Press, Great Barrington, MA, 1990.

Morter, M. Ted, *Dynamic Health* by B.E.S.T. Research, Inc., Rogers, AR, 1995.

Pearce, Joseph C., *Magical Child: Rediscovering Nature's Plan for our Children,* Bantam Books, New York, 1980.

Stone, Randolph, *Dr. Randolph Stone's Polarity Therapy: The Complete Collected Works,* Vol. I (1986) and Vol. II (1987), CRCS Publications.

Strickland, Rennard, *Tonto's Revenge: Reflections on American Indian Culture and Policy,* University of New Mexico Press, Albuquerque, 1997.

Upledger, John E., *Craniosacral Therapy II: Beyond the Dura,* Eastland Press, Seattle, 1987.

Zaren, Ananda, *Materia Medica: Core Elements of the Materia Medica of the Mind,* Ulrich Burgdorf Homeopathic Publishing House, Göttingen, Germany, 1993.